M-16 CRAS
COURS

Kenny Dallas & Tim Sexton

M-46 *CRASH COURSE*

DADS FIGHTING FOR THE HEARTS OF THEIR CHILDREN

DAVID **C** COOK

transforming lives together

M46 CRASH COURSE PARTICIPANT'S GUIDE
Published by David C Cook
4050 Lee Vance Drive
Colorado Springs, CO 80918 U.S.A.

Integrity Music Limited, a Division of David C Cook
Brighton, East Sussex BN1 2RE, England

The graphic circle C logo is a registered trademark of David C Cook.

The website addresses recommended throughout this book are offered as a
resource to you. These websites are not intended in any way to be or imply an
endorsement on the part of David C Cook, nor do we vouch for their content.

ISBN 978-0-8307-8130-0
eISBN 978-0-8307-8131-7

© 2020 The M46 Revolution, Inc.

The Team: Michael Covington, Jeff Gerke,
Michael Fedison, Jon Middel, Susan Murdock
Cover Design: James Hershberger

Printed in the United States of America
First Edition 2020

1 2 3 4 5 6 7 8 9 10

083120

DEDICATION

From Kenny

To my wife, Shannon: Asking you to marry me was the best decision I have ever made. From the day I met you in the sixth grade to when we started dating in the eleventh grade, through six kids and twenty-six years of marriage and until now … you truly are a Proverbs 31 woman and my "warrior." I love you with all my heart!

To my children, Jacob, Caleb, Joshua, David, Elly, and Zech: "Like arrows in the hands of a warrior are children born in one's youth. Blessed is the man whose quiver is full of them." My life is truly blessed and full of joy because of each of you. I am so proud to be your dad. I love each of you with all my heart!

From Tim

To my wife, Georgia—my warrior! God placed you in my life to tether me to something solid while I thrashed around trying to grow up. I wasn't ready for you, and I surely wasn't ready to be a dad. But God is good. He has taught us both how to love each other, and He has blessed us beyond measure. You are my best friend and a tangible rock that we all count on every day. I am so thankful that you are the mother of our children. You are true and faithful, and your love for Jesus inspires me. I love you.

To our four boys, Joshua, Jordan, Jesse, and Ezra: I am so thankful for all of you. I am blessed to be your dad, and I love this season of life where I get to watch you all as men. I couldn't be more proud, and you are the greatest legacy a dad could hope for. I love you all.

CONTENTS

Included with this participant's
guide is free access to the M46
online videos and leader's guide.
Visit ***www.m46dads.com/season1***.

ACKNOWLEDGMENTS

To our board of directors: Clifton Youngblood, Robbie Moore, Mike Holmes, Jay Kimsey, Les Lambert, and Mark Hall. Thank you all for your support, encouragement, friendship, and wisdom over the years. None of this would have been possible without you. Each of you is a true man of God and an image-bearer of the one true King!

To the men of Eagles Landing and Trinity, thank you! Thank you for being a part of our first CRASH Communities. Thank you for being real, transparent, and faithful. Thank you for being men who desire to fight for the hearts of your children!

INTRODUCTION

"And he will turn the hearts of fathers to their children
and the hearts of children to their fathers."

Malachi 4:6a

When I (Kenny) met Tim Sexton years ago, I instantly knew we would be friends.

I'd just listened to Tim speak for the first time, and I already knew we had a handful of things in common. We both loved the Lord and wanted to honor Him with our lives. We both had big families we adored. And there was also one other major thing that drew me to him: we both had lived long enough to experience some real "failure" in our lives, failure that had taught us to truly appreciate the depths of God's goodness, His powerful redeeming grace, and His fierce love for us.

Tim and I were imperfect dads whose lives had been transformed by the power of the gospel.

The first offstage words I ever heard Tim say (and I heard him from across a crowded room) were, "We've got to be loud about our sin and even louder about our King." Yeah, this was definitely a guy I had to get to know. And so I did.

As our friendship progressed, we realized that we'd come to the same conclusion about our failures: that at the end of our self-reliance was surrender.

Jesus speaks of daily "dying to self," but Tim and I discussed how that process can be so *ugly* because of the baggage we carry in our flesh, but also how *beautiful* it can be as we trust Jesus and find our true identity in Christ alone. It is truly at that point that the gospel begins to speak into every area of our lives.

As we talked, a dream started to take shape. Because of our shared experiences, we imagined creating a place where men like us could go and, even in the midst of their failures and struggles, be transparent. And get support from others on the same path.

So often, we show up to church and act like nothing is wrong. We put on our best clothes, best shoes, and best face to make everyone believe that everything is *great*! Tim and I wanted to create a place where men didn't have to pretend that they "had it all together."

If you're reading this book, then you know the pressures of trying to succeed both at work and at home. It's hard enough to be "successful" at work, but being a good father is probably the hardest thing a man will ever do. Tim and I didn't want to be just good daddies—we also wanted to be godly daddies who intentionally pointed their kids toward Christ.

Tim and I began to discuss questions like, "Where can a man go and be honest about his fears and struggles as a dad?" and "Where can a guy go to be encouraged and equipped to be the daddy he wants to be?" We laughed as we realized that what we were really looking for was an AA meeting for dads! A place where we could show up and say, "My name is Kenny Dallas. I love my kids, and I want to honor the Lord, but this fatherhood thing is *hard* and I need some help!"

In the winter of 2015, we launched Operation M46 (now called M46 Dads) for the men in our church and school community. The mission of M46 was simply to inspire and equip dads to fight for the hearts of their children. We sent out invitations that asked, "Do you want to be a better dad?"

The response was overwhelming. We decided to meet the first Friday of every month at 6:30 a.m. At our first meeting, the place was *packed*, and every month thereafter, the room was filled with men who had these things in common: 1) they wanted to honor the

Lord, 2) they loved their families and wanted to be the best daddies they could be, and 3) they had figured out that this fatherhood thing was hard.

Many of these men had their own stories of personal or professional failure, but the common bond was that they all were hungry to be better equipped to fight for the hearts of their children.

Every session, we focused on one main verse of Scripture, equipped men with one tool they could use in their parenting, provided them with one visual image to help remember the lesson, and then sent them out the door with one "challenge" to go *do* with their children.

Our motto is that we are dads who are fighting for the hearts of our children.

Did you know that 74 percent of men say they are not equipped to be the type of dad they want to be?[1] Barna research has shown that 89 percent of men feel inadequate in training their children.

With our dads meetings, we had hit on something desperately needed—a place where a man could be honest, transparent, and real. A place where a dad would be inspired and equipped to fight for the heart of his children. Over the last five-plus years, Tim and I have been leading groups of men through the curriculum of M46 Dads. We are extremely excited that it is available to put into your hands today.

WHY M46?

The term M46 comes from the very last verse in the Old Testament, Malachi 4:6, which says, "And he will turn the hearts of fathers to their children and the hearts of children to their fathers."

Malachi 4:6 … M46.

When it was written, the *he* in this verse referred to the prophet Elijah. We know from Jesus that it also points to John the Baptist (Matt. 17:12), whom Scripture says came in the spirit and power of Elijah (Luke 1:17). While we acknowledge that this verse has a specific focus in the history of salvation, we also believe that, when God's power is unleashed in families and nations, it really does draw the hearts of fathers and children together.

It is essential that every man understands that God is with him as he turns toward Christ and fights for the hearts of his children. This verse communicates the love, blessing, favor, hope, redemption, unity, and legacy that God offers to us as His sons. And in return, we can offer those to our children.

WHAT M46 IS NOT

The M46 CRASH Course participant's guide you have in your hands, together with the video series that goes with it, is the culmination of five years of M46 meetings with fathers just like you. Before we tell you what to expect, let me start by telling you what this workbook is *not*:

- This workbook is *not* about making you feel shame or guilt from past mistakes. We are just going to go ahead and assume that you are an imperfect man who has your own unique story and situation that probably includes some regret over past decisions and anxiety about what the future holds. It is time for your past to define you no longer!

- This workbook is *not* written by parenting "gurus" and is *not* a 1-2-3, step-by-step process for producing perfect children. This book is written *by* regular men *to* regular men who believe the gospel can speak into any situation we may face as fathers.

- This workbook is *not* intended to be a Bible study or homework. We've included a ton of good stuff here, but you don't have to do any of it. You are encouraged to go through every part of this workbook, but we urge you to use it as much or as little as you want. It's designed to free you up, not tie you down.

WHAT M46 IS

- This workbook *is* going to inspire you. You will read stories of successes ... right alongside stories of failure. You'll read stories from history, and you'll get examples of M46 Moments—stories of how the hearts of fathers and children were turned toward one another. We are including these stories to encourage you through what has happened in the lives of other men, but also to challenge you that your story is still being written.

- This workbook *is* going to equip you with more "tools" for your tool chest. By *tools* we mean scriptural principles that will guide your parenting. At the beginning, a man has in his tool chest only those tools that his father gave him. Maybe that's enough and maybe it isn't. Why do you need to be equipped by something like M46? Because you cannot give what you do not have.

- This workbook *is* going to challenge you to intentionally fight for the hearts of your children. Every chapter concludes with a challenge for you to take action. We would love it if you made a commitment right now to learn every tool and complete every challenge, even if you don't read every page of this workbook. You with us?

HOW TO USE THIS WORKBOOK

In the Old Testament book of Joshua, we read about how God dried up the Jordan River so His people could cross it in order to begin their conquest of the Promised Land. While they were crossing the suddenly dry riverbed, God instructed them to pick up stones and stack them on the far bank (see Josh. 4). The stones would be a reminder of the Lord's faithfulness. God told them that one day their children would see the monument and ask, "What do these stones mean?" and they could tell the wonderful works of God.

We believe that going through the M46 Dads program is going to be monumental in your life, as well. Not because we are incredible teachers, but because we believe that the powerful promise and truth God gave in Malachi 4:6 is for you and your family. At the end of this journey, we want you to have river stones piled up, so one day you can open this journal and read to your children some stories of the faithfulness of God to you and your family.

We hope you'll be getting together with a group of men to view the videos—in person or online—whether you go through the pages of this workbook on your own or not. (Go to **www.m46dads.com/season1** to view the videos.) At a minimum, make sure to bring your workbook with you every time you meet. We encourage you to take notes in it from the video teaching, write out the new tool you learned, and record the details of how your challenge went with each of your children.

As far as how often you'll be meeting with your group, that's flexible. We don't know if you'll be watching videos once a week, once a month, once a quarter, or once a day. But we have designed this workbook to be full of resources to help you employ the tool you'll learn and succeed with the challenge we give you each time. Each chapter is to be used between video sessions.

For each chapter, you'll find:

1. A section that examines what is already in your tool chest about that topic ... things you learned from your father, your culture, and so on.

2. A powerful word from Tim on how to see and understand the topic through the lens of the gospel.

3. A section on exactly what you plan to pass down to your children about that topic. We men make plans for everything: a business plan, a retirement plan, a plan for what to buy at the grocery store. But what about a plan for how we are going to train our children in specific areas?

4. A *challenge* from Kenny on what this could look like practically for your family.

5. A section that will prepare you for the next session.

We have made this as dad-friendly as we can. We have laid out this workbook for you to use as much or as little as you want, as we've said. We have organized every section so that it is in almost the same order every time, so you can flip to the exact sections you want to look at. We have even given you a bunch of space to write your thoughts, questions, and stories as they come to your mind.

A RHINO IN THE WILD

One last thing: Why the heck does this workbook have a rhino on the front cover? We use the rhino for three reasons:

1. Rhinos are *humongous* animals.

Whether you have been a good dad or a bad dad, whether you have been present or absent, whether you are living in the home with your kids or you live in another country, *you are humongous in the life of your child.*

Proverbs 17:6 says, "The glory of children is their fathers." At least when children are of a certain age, they rejoice in their fathers. They idolize their fathers. It's in our DNA to want to be in close relationship with our father. Believe it or not—deserve it or not—your kids feel this way toward you. How will you intentionally use this influence?

> 2. While a rhino can run thirty miles per hour, it
> can see only thirty feet in front of itself.

Do you know why a rhino has that huge horn on its head and armor-plated skin? Because it is going to run into stuff! An African rhino can weigh up to 3,100 pounds, and yet it can run at speeds of up to thirty miles per hour. You don't stop a galloping 1.55-ton armored beast on a dime. If it happens to be running along and something gets in its way inside thirty feet ... well, that's why it has that horn and plated skin.

If a rhino is going to run at all, it has to run by *faith*, not by *sight*. Now, who does that sound like?

My brother, you are going to make some mistakes along the way—maybe big ones. But you have to keep running by faith for the sake of your family.

> 3. Finally, what do you call a group of birds? A flock.
> What do you call a group of fish? A school. Do you
> know what you call a group of rhinos? A *crash*.

Can you think of a better name than *crash* to describe a group of men getting together to be better equipped as fathers and sent to action? That's why we call an M46 meeting a CRASH. No matter how often your CRASH chooses to meet, what matters is that you run together.[2]

CHARGE FORWARD

So, rhino dad, what if the promise of Malachi 4:6 is true for you and your children? What if God is standing by to bend the power of the universe to turn your heart toward your kids and to turn your kids' hearts to you?

Will you complete all nine sessions? Will you complete all nine challenges? What could your relationship with your children look like at the end of these nine sessions?

For the sake of your children, it is time to get up and start running by faith.

WELCOME TO M46 DADS
Dads Fighting for the Hearts of Their Children

CRASH 1

THE FINISH LINE

Dear rhino dad, have these pages open during the CRASH.

PRE-CRASH PREPARATION

Today's CRASH will equip you with the Tool of Proper Perspective. To get the most out of today's CRASH:

1. If possible, silence your phone and put it away. Focus your full attention on being equipped to be the dad your children deserve.

2. Make sure you are fully present by saying a short prayer simply asking the Lord to clear your mind and give you "ears to hear" what you need today to prepare you to lead your family.

3. Be open and transparent with other men at your CRASH. Receive the help you need from another dad and/or provide encouragement to another dad as you both walk this fatherhood journey.

TABLE TIME

Write down the names of the men in your group and some things you hope to get out of today's CRASH.

What came up in the discussion that you'd like to commit to pray about? Anything you can do to encourage one of the men at your table?

VIDEO NOTES

As you watch today's video (www.m46dads.com/season1), write down the main points.

IMAGE

The following image is provided to help you remember the main principle of this session and also to help you reteach this to your children or friends.

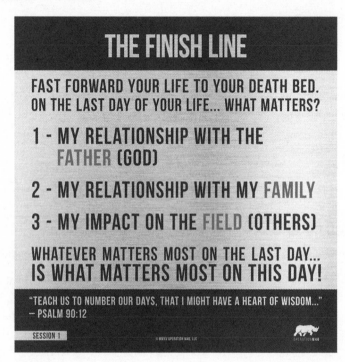

KEY SCRIPTURE

"Teach us to number our days, that we may gain a heart of wisdom."
Psalm 90:12 (NIV)

Paraphrase the passage in your own words.

THE TOOL

Each CRASH, we're putting a new tool in your hands. A tool is a principle that can guide your parenting.

In this first session, you have been handed the Tool of Proper Perspective. In this session, you were asked to fast-forward your life to the very end ... till you are eighty, ninety, one hundred years old. Imagine that you are lying on your deathbed and you know that tonight you will reach the end of your life and come face-to-face with the Lord. In that moment, ask yourself this simple question: What matters?

> 1. What matters in terms of my relationship with God (FATHER)?
> 2. What matters in terms of my relationship with those closest to me (FAMILY)?
> 3. What matters in terms of the impact I have on others (FIELD)?

Asking ourselves this question can provide tremendous clarity to our lives. It provides us with a *proper perspective* on what truly matters. Remember: whatever truly matters on the last day is what truly matters on this day.

THE CHALLENGE

Dad, you are the most influential man in your child's life. In this session, we established *what matters* ... Father, Family, and Field.

CRASH COURSE 1

Dear rhino dad, use the following pages to help you dig deeper into this session and record the challenge as you fight for the hearts of your children. Go through them at your own pace or just pick and choose which to do.

> *"Life is like a coin. You can spend it any way*
> *you wish, but you only spend it once."*
> Lillian Dickson

THE HEART OF A RHINO

The Greek king Pyrrhus saw himself as being the next Alexander the Great. In 280 BC, Pyrrhus brought an army of 25,000 men and twenty war elephants to invade Italy. He led his men to victory in both the Battle of Heraclea and the Battle of Asculum. With the victories, Pyrrhus had established his foothold in Italy, but at great cost.

The price of his victories was the loss of over 7,500 men, many of his generals, and a good number of his elite fighters. Pyrrhus is reported to have said, "If we are victorious in one more battle with the Romans, we shall be utterly ruined." In 275 BC, the "successful" warrior king called off the campaign and took his troops back to Greece.

It is from King Pyrrhus that we get the term *pyrrhic victory,* which means a goal that is achieved but at too great a cost.

Jesus said it another way: "For what does it profit a man to gain the whole world and forfeit his soul?" (Mark 8:36).

Rhino dad, what would it profit you to gain the whole world (money, fame, power) and forfeit your children?

The principle of this lesson is the Tool of Proper Perspective. As we live our lives, as we make decisions, as we set our time priorities, let's regularly ask ourselves, "What matters?"

DIGGING DEEPER

In the video, we used the analogy of running a race. The Tool of Proper Perspective is as important for a dad as it is for a runner to know his finish line. If you don't know your finish line, you may run hard and you may run fast, but you will *never* have the confidence that you are running in the right direction.

Be honest and answer the following questions …

If "What Matters" is your finish line, what is the finish line you're racing toward?

What stands in the way of your finish line?

In considering "What Matters," list some things that did *not* come to mind.

Be careful with that last question. Just because something does not come to mind doesn't mean it is necessarily a distraction that needs to be eliminated. For instance, I have never heard a man on his deathbed say that he cares how big a house he had, what type of car he drove, or that he wishes he could have spent a couple more hours at the office away from his family. But that obviously does not mean that jobs or possessions do not matter in any sense at all. It's just that they matter and have value only in terms of how they affect my relationship with God, my family, or my impact on others.

Having the Tool of Proper Perspective helps me understand that my job and possessions are important because they give me the opportunity to honor the Lord (Father), provide for my loved ones (Family), and impact others (Field).

By the way, what is more important: time or money? I once heard a man answer that question in this way: "That's easy. Time is much more important, because money can be replaced, but time cannot!"

It is so true that many men have gone bankrupt multiple times in their lives and still ended up as millionaires. In contrast, there is a sacredness to time. Once a day is over, I can never get it back.

Lillian Dickson said, "Life is like a coin. You can spend it any way you wish, but you only spend it once." The Tool of Proper Perspective serves as a compass. Regardless of what direction we travel or where we go, the compass will always point us back to what truly matters, to help guide our daily choices of how to spend our time.

Looking at your list of what matters and what does not, what needs to change in your life?

RHINO COLLISION
Examining your own heart

LEARNED FROM MY DAD

Dads are not only teaching their children how to live life, but they also are "painting a picture" of God with their daily actions. The same is true in your relationship with your own dad.

As we think about the Tool of Proper Perspective, let's take a look at what your father taught you.

Ask yourself the following questions and be brutally honest.

This isn't about bashing your father. He did the best he could with what *he* had been given. This is about calling things what they are and assessing the toolbox we walked into fatherhood carrying.

What did your dad teach you about Proper Perspective?

What did your father *not* teach you about Proper Perspective?

LEARNED FROM MY CULTURE

Colossians 2:8 (NIV) commands us, "See to it that no one takes you captive through hollow and deceptive philosophy, which depends on human tradition and the elemental spiritual forces of this world rather than on Christ."

We are shaped not only by what we were taught by our father. We are also tremendously impacted by our culture. Ask yourself the following questions and be brutally honest.

What does our culture say should be a man's finish line? What does everyone seem to be racing for? Riches? Fame? Impact? Legacy? Political correctness and having the "right" views on issues that are important to the culture right now?

What does our culture say should be a dad's role regarding "faith, family, and field"?

What messages have you received about a father's role in "faith, family, and field" from the church or from Christians?

A WORD FROM PASTOR TIM

You have to know where you're trying to go before you take off running. And it's real easy for us as men to get busy in our careers; provide for our families; push our kids academically, morally, or athletically; and navigate all the land mines of this life while forgetting to check our compass. Before you know it, we're way off target.

I know this may sound morbid, but I wonder what will be said at my funeral. I've been to funerals where golf clubs were literally propped up against the casket. I've discovered that the guy we were there to honor was a big Notre Dame fan. Nothing wrong with those things, but I doubt that any of us will be thinking of golf or college football when we're on our deathbeds.

One of the tragedies of our fast-paced, microwavable, everything-at-your-fingertips, google-it society is that we just don't stop long enough to consider what really matters. And if we do consider it, how many will actually do anything about it? As men, sometimes we recognize that we're not making, in the lives of the people we love, the investments we say we want to make. But it's so easy to brush those thoughts aside and just keep busy.

M46 Dads is primarily about being intentional. The legacy we hope to leave won't happen by accident. And when it comes to our children, we have a limited amount of time to influence them. Our legacy is formed by the choices we make. Do we really want to be remembered just for our hobbies or occupation?

For a short time when I was in sales, I worked in the medical field. I often encountered families that were dealing with end-of-life questions. Occasionally, I had to watch families tear one another apart over the assets left behind by a loved one. But once in a while, I got to witness the impact of a life lived for the sake of the gospel. The contrast was stark.

In the end, what matters is the mark we leave on the souls in our care. You don't want to leave your loved ones and your friends fighting over your stuff. You want them telling stories about how you gave your life away for their good and for the sake of the gospel.

REWRITING YOUR STORY

Romans 12:2 commands us, "Do not be conformed to this world, but be transformed by the renewal of your mind, that by testing you may discern what is the will of God, what is good and acceptable and perfect."

When bad habits or false pictures of God get handed down from father to son, it's almost automatic that those same things will be handed down to *that* dad's children. That is what some refer to as a generational curse. It will keep going that way until someone decides to be a cycle breaker.

Scripture also makes it clear that the opposite is possible too. We can hand down righteousness that will impact generation upon generation, as well. That's a generational *blessing*.

Regardless of what your father gave you and what your culture has handed to you, you can be a cycle breaker for good. It's time to be *intentional* about what you will pass down to your children.

How are you doing on the Tool of Proper Perspective with your own children? Are you doing with your kids what your dad did with you or what culture has taught you? Describe how that's going.

What, if anything, would you like to change in what you're showing them that matters most in life?

A father paints a picture of God in the minds of his children. But if Dad is painting with an angry brush or a selfish brush or an uncaring brush, what picture of God is he producing? This isn't about bashing your father—it's about understanding yourself. On this topic of proper perspective, what kind of brush are you using and what kind of picture of God are you painting for your kids?

How do you react to this sentence: "To be a better dad, you need God to be bigger in your heart and in your house"?

In what ways might God become bigger in your heart and house?

RHINO CHARGE

Fighting for the hearts of your children

RUNNING BY FAITH

As we've seen, rhinos can run up to thirty miles per hour, but they can see only thirty feet ahead. They have that giant horn and armor-plated skin because they are going to make some mistakes along the way and crash into stuff. The bottom line is that if they are going to run, they are going to run by faith and not by sight.

Christian dads are just like that. We're going to make many mistakes too. But, also like rhinos, we are not alone.

> *"See what kind of love the Father has given to us, that we should be called children of God; and so we are."*
>
> 1 John 3:1

Our heavenly Father has not left us to figure life out by ourselves. He is with us! We encourage you to read the Bible, think about God, and ask Him to reveal ways you can apply this to your life. What power do you have if God is with you as you fight for the hearts of your children?

Use the space below these Scripture references to record what the Lord shows you.

Psalm 39:4–5

Mark 8:36

Psalm 144:1–4

James 4:13–17

Psalm 90:12

A WORD FROM COACH KENNY

Rhino dad, I don't know about you, but I don't want to live a life of regret. I don't want to get to the end of my days and wish I had lived differently.

Here is the cold, hard truth: whatever mistakes you and I have made in the past are real and have consequences, but with God's grace, they do not have to define our future. You cannot change yesterday, but God has given each of us the precious gift of *today*. Drink in the absolute wisdom of this verse: "Teach us to number our days, that we may gain a heart of wisdom" (Ps. 90:12 NIV).

It is time for me to be dead honest with you: Tim and I don't want you to "enjoy" this CRASH course. Well, we want you to have a good time and all. But if that's all that happens, we'll be disappointed.

You need to know that we are praying that M46 will absolutely *ignite a revolution*. A revolution not only in your family, but also in your community and world!

A revolution is the physical overthrow of a current social order. The current social order today is not just fatherless homes. It also includes homes where there is a man present, but it has become a visionless home.

Barna Research shows that 89 percent of men do not feel adequate to train their children the way they want to.[3] I meet men all the time who obviously want to be the best daddies they can be. It's not that men don't want to be the spiritual leaders of their homes … it's that they simply are not equipped. They don't have good tools in their tool chest.

Tim and I believe that Scripture calls a husband to be the primary spiritual leader of the home. We want you to know that M46 Dads is here to equip you. Starting with this session and for the next eight sessions, our desire is to inspire and equip you to live a life that truly matters … one in which you are equipped to fight for the hearts of your children.

In this lesson, you have defined your finish line and learned that the only things that will matter on your last day will be Father, Family, and Field.

Make sure you get this truth too: *if those things are all that will matter on the last day, then they are all that matter today.*

What would your life look like if you started running with a crystal-clear finish line? How would your behavior change if all your decisions were made through the lens of the Tool of Proper Perspective? How would that impact your family?

Many people sit around waiting for revival to break out in churches across the nation. But what if, instead of waiting to see revival happen in our churches, men began to intentionally fight for the hearts of their children? What if the next Great Awakening doesn't happen primarily in church buildings across the nation, but rather in living rooms all across the world as men intentionally turn their hearts toward their children as the spiritual leaders of their homes?

Men, it is time to quit talking and to start taking action. It is time to ignite a revolution in your home, your community, your nation, and your world. It begins by clearly knowing *what matters*.

Rhino dad: on your mark, get set, *go*.

M46 MOMENT

My (Kenny's) father is my mentor. He is my sacred counselor, and he is a trusted friend. There is no one I love, respect, and trust more than him. But our relationship was not always like that. In fact, for many years our relationship was very much the opposite.

My mom and dad got married right out of high school. By the time they were twenty-one, they already had my brother and me. That year, they got divorced.

Both of my parents ended up remarrying, having two more children apiece, and living an hour away from each other. As a kid, you don't realize how hard life can be for adults. I couldn't comprehend the complexities of my dad living an hour away, of him having a new family, and of him working the graveyard shift. The only thing I knew was that I didn't get to see my dad very often. At first, I wasn't mad. But I did carry an unspoken sadness. Over time, the sadness became bitterness.

The summer after I graduated high school, I went to a Fourth of July celebration at a church. I had grown up with my mom taking me to church, but for some reason that night when the gospel was presented, I felt like the pastor was speaking only to me. At the end of his talk, he asked if anyone wanted to put their faith in Christ, be baptized, or surrender their lives to ministry.

I raised my hand for all of it. I was all in!

As I began to read my Bible, I came across the Lord's Prayer. A part of it reads, "Forgive us our sins, as we have forgiven those who sin against us" (Matt. 6:12 NLT). The notes at the bottom of the page in my study Bible said that Jesus was communicating that God will forgive our sins in the same manner that we forgive others. In that moment, I knew I had to forgive my dad and get rid of the deep bitterness and resentment that had built up in my heart.

In my last year in college, I saw that the Promise Keepers men's movement had an event scheduled in Memphis at the Liberty Bowl. I asked my dad if he would go with me, and he agreed. As soon as the first speaker finished his presentation about the power of the gospel, my father turned to me and said he needed to talk. With tears in his eyes, he told me he knew that he wasn't around much as I grew up. He asked me if I would forgive him.

I don't know exactly what happened to cause my dad to ask for forgiveness, but in that moment, my heart was turned toward my father. I absolutely and completely forgave him.

Many years later, I read the promise in Malachi 4:6: "He will turn the hearts of fathers to their children and the hearts of children to their fathers." I discovered that this verse is actually a promise of what happens through the gospel. It's *exactly* what happened to my dad and me.

In that divine appointment with my father, God completely redeemed a broken relationship. Our heavenly Father began to lead us together down a path to a new relationship in which, over time, my dad would become my mentor and trusted counselor. Today, he is the man I look up to more than anyone else in this world.

THE CHALLENGE: FIGHT FOR THEIR HEARTS!

"In the future, when your children ask you,
'What do these stones mean?' tell them."

Joshua 4:6–7a (NIV)

Document your challenge here. The more detailed you are, the more you will be able to look back and tell your children the story of God's faithfulness in your life.

Rhino dad, you are the most influential man in your child's life. In this session, we established *what matters* … Father, Family, and Field.

Under each of those three words, list out three things:

1. A specific goal you want to accomplish
2. Any obstacle that is standing in the way of completing that goal
3. A scripture—God's truth—that encourages and supports you in overcoming the obstacle to arrive at your goal

For example, if under "Father" you write down "Have a closer relationship with God," and yet your obstacle is "I struggle to believe He has forgiven my sin," then find a Bible verse that supports your goal. For this one, you might select Ephesians 1:7–8: "He is so rich in kindness and grace that he purchased our freedom with the blood of his Son and forgave our sins. He has showered his kindness on us, along with all wisdom and understanding" (NLT). You can use a website or app to help you, such as Bible Gateway or YouVersion Bible, by typing in keywords to look up connected verses.

Pick one of these goals to try to make headway on between now and the next CRASH.

If you are part of a CRASH Community, bring this CRASH Course workbook with you to the next meeting (or take a picture of these pages on your phone for reference). Be ready to share and discuss with your Christian brothers.

Fight for the hearts of your children

FATHER	FAMILY	FIELD
Goal 1:	Goal 1:	Goal 1:
Obstacle:	Obstacle:	Obstacle:
Scripture:	Scripture:	Scripture:
Goal 2:	Goal 2:	Goal 2:
Obstacle:	Obstacle:	Obstacle:
Scripture:	Scripture:	Scripture:

CRASH 2

THE COVENANT

Dear rhino dad, have these pages open during the CRASH.

PRE-CRASH PREPARATION

Today's CRASH will equip you with the Tool of Unconditional Love. To get the most out of today's CRASH:

1. Before you get to the meeting place, or as you're waiting for the CRASH to begin, flip back through the previous pages. Remind yourself what we talked about, reread what notes you wrote, and refresh your mind about how the challenge went.

2. If possible, silence your phone and put it away. Focus your full attention on being equipped to be the dad your children deserve.

3. Make sure you are fully present by saying a short prayer simply asking the Lord to clear your mind and give you "ears to hear" what you need today to prepare you to lead your family.

4. Be open and transparent with other men at your CRASH. Receive the help you need from another

dad and/or provide encouragement to another dad
as you both walk this fatherhood journey.

REVIEW AND TABLE TIME

Write down some of the main points from last session's review.

What came up in the discussion that you'd like to commit to pray
about? Anything you can do to encourage one of the men at your table?

VIDEO NOTES

As you watch today's video, write down the main points.

IMAGE

The following image is provided to help you remember the main principle of this session and also to help you reteach this to your children or friends.

KEY SCRIPTURE

"He entered once for all into the holy places, not by means of the blood of goats and calves but by means of his own blood, thus securing an eternal redemption."
Hebrews 9:12

Paraphrase the passage in your own words.

THE TOOL

Each CRASH, we're putting a new tool in your hands. A tool is a principle that can guide your parenting.

In the second CRASH, you have been handed the Tool of Unconditional Love. In this session, we want to help you see and understand, from God's Word, the depth of His unconditional love for His children.

Once you see just how comprehensive Jesus' finished work on the cross truly is, you'll be better equipped to hand that gospel down to your children. If you can communicate and demonstrate to your children that there is nothing they can do to make you love them more or less, you are modeling God's covenant love for His children.

The goal is that your children will begin to understand that God has already done every single thing that needs to be done in order for them to be made right with Him and to be kept right with Him.

THE CHALLENGE

Rhino dad, you are the most influential man in your child's life. This session was about God's incredible proactive love for His people, and how as dads we get to communicate and demonstrate that love to our children.

CRASH COURSE 2

Dear rhino dad, use the following pages to help you dig deeper into this session and record the challenge as you fight for the hearts of your children. Go through them at your own pace or just pick and choose which to do.

> *"This is now a covenant of pure grace; let no*
> *man attempt to mix works with it."*
>
> Charles Spurgeon

THE HEART OF A RHINO

Eric Liddell was immortalized in the 1981 film *Chariots of Fire,* which is based on the Scottish sprinter's gold medal run in the 1924 Olympics. You can probably remember the main song from the soundtrack too. But that movie really didn't do his life justice.

Liddell famously refused to run on Sundays because of his faith. That meant he would miss his best event, the 100-meter race. He ran in the 400-meter dash instead and won the gold medal. He wasn't even expected to place in that race. But he treated the whole 400 meters like a sprint, and he broke the world record. When asked about the race, he said, "I run the first 200 meters as hard as I can. Then, for the second 200 meters, with God's help, I run harder."

Eric Liddell left home in 1925, the year after he won the gold, to become a missionary in China. His friends couldn't believe he wanted to go to a faraway land and miss out on an opportunity to capitalize on his fame and win even more gold in the 1928 Olympics.

He would have been a favorite to win. But his love for the people of China and his desire for them to hear the gospel was far greater than his need for more fame.

For several years, Liddell served as both a science and sports teacher at a college in China. But war broke out when the Japanese invaded China in 1937. In what is now known as the Rape of Nanking, the Japanese massacred as many as 300,000 Chinese civilians. Liddell was undeterred. He refused to use bodyguards when visiting the sick, because relying on a gun instead of God wasn't his way. He fed the poor, ministered to the sick, and defied the Japanese.

As the war worsened, Liddell eventually sent his pregnant wife and two daughters home to England and vowed to join them later. He did briefly visit home, and his friends were stunned when he decided to return to China even as the war spiraled out of control.

Liddell was captured by the Japanese in March 1943 and sent to an internment camp in Weihsien. Those who knew him in that prison camp described him as nearly selfless, always caring for the needs of others, daily sacrificing for the needs of those in the internment camp with him, and always walking in great humility. He literally gave his life away for the sake of the gospel.

Winston Churchill even secured Liddell's release, but Liddell made a pregnant woman in the camp take his place. Reading his story is like reading about a modern-day knight. Liddell lived in a way that set him apart from everyone around him, even in those extreme circumstances. He was clearly willing to give his life for the sake of the Chinese people. Those who knew him knew his convictions weren't borne of cold, religious piety but of a love that came from his love for God.

To boost the morale of the prisoners, Liddell once agreed to run a race with others in the camp. He was terribly sick at the time. He had lost an incredible amount of weight, and no one knew he was suffering from a brain tumor. He ran anyway. He sprinted out to an early lead, but his legs began to fail him. He came in second. But the inspiration he provided that day rippled through generations afterward.

On February 21, 1945, just a few months before the camp was liberated, Eric Liddell died. His daughter Maureen never even met her father.

You could say Eric Liddell is one of my heroes.

I got to share Eric's story with my son on a long drive in the car recently. He seemed to be nearly as captivated as I was by this man's life. I want my son to know about men like Eric Liddell. Stories like this, real ones, can help me as a dad paint a clearer picture of God for my son—and anchor him to a real definition of manhood too.

But this story also points to a God who loves us even more perfectly. Jesus also left His home, though He didn't have to. He sacrificed everything for an ungrateful people. He truly did everything for the sake of others. Then He suffered and died so that we can go home.

Rhino dad, fight for the hearts of your children by pointing them to what matters eternally, and to what real courage and sacrifice look like.

> *"Since it is so likely that children will meet cruel enemies, let them at least have heard of brave knights and heroic courage."*
> C. S. Lewis

DIGGING DEEPER

Maybe you grew up having a clear understanding of the gospel. But undoubtedly there will be men reading this who, like me, grew up believing they were never quite measuring up to God's standards. So long as we hold that belief, intimacy with God is going to be virtually impossible.

Of course we're not measuring up to God's standard. That's why Jesus had to live the perfect life and die on our behalf.

What motivates you to try to live the Christian life?

What do you believe is God's reaction or response when you fail?

What does the perfect life of Jesus, and the cross, mean to you?

Rhino dad, one of the things that has become crystal clear to us over the years is that dads assume their children know they love them unconditionally. But in our desire to push our kids toward success, academic excellence, or athletic achievements, we can easily send the message that they are incapable of meeting our standards.

Remember, we are painting a picture of what God is like for our children to see. Also remember that there is an enemy who would love nothing more than to convince your children that God's standards are just too high and that He is angry or disappointed that we have failed Him yet again.

What a tragedy. What a mockery of the cross and all that was accomplished there.

RHINO COLLISION
Examining your own heart

LEARNED FROM MY DAD

Dads are teaching their children how to live, but they are also "painting a picture of God" with their daily actions. The same is true in your relationship with your own dad.

As we think about the Tool of Unconditional Love, let's take a look at what your father taught you. Ask yourself the following questions and be brutally honest.

This isn't about bashing your father. He did the best he could with what *he* had been given. This is about calling things what they are and assessing the toolbox we walked into fatherhood carrying.

How did your father communicate and demonstrate unconditional love?

How did your father at times communicate or demonstrate a consumer-type love?

What do you think you learned about the character of God from your father?

LEARNED FROM MY CULTURE

Colossians 2:8 (NIV) commands us, "See to it that no one takes you captive through hollow and deceptive philosophy, which depends on human tradition and the elemental spiritual forces of this world rather than on Christ."

We are shaped not only by what we were taught by our father but also by our culture. Ask yourself the following questions and be brutally honest.

What do we learn about love from our culture (Hollywood, TV, music, etc.)?

How does our culture say that a man should express love?

What messages have you received about the gospel, how God looks at you, and what His expectations are of you from the church or from Christians?

A WORD FROM PASTOR TIM

Rhino dad, let's be honest: we have a pretty daunting task before us. We want to love our children well, but we also have to discipline and teach them. We all want to see our children do well and learn responsibility. We don't want them to be a burden to others when they grow up. We want them to know how to work hard, and we want them to treat others well.

At the same time, you also want them to know and love God. You want them to understand His character, and you want them to obey Him. So often, it feels like we're being counterproductive and maybe even sending mixed messages to our kids. But it's so incredibly important, if we want them to know, love, and obey God, that they understand what really happened to them when they got saved. They have to know the God who took the penalty and the curse and left for us the blessing of eternal life and access to God, and even friendship with Him.

If you want your kids to learn to trust and obey God—in reality, not just when others are watching—then you want them to *love* God and not fear Him.

The fuel that will give your children the will and the strength to be the people you want them to be actually comes from them knowing that all of God's expectations for them have already been met in His Son.

Their standing before God is based on His Son's performance, not their own.

REWRITING YOUR STORY

Regardless of what your father gave you and what your culture has handed to you, you can be a cycle breaker for good. It's time to be *intentional* about what you will pass down to your children.

How are you doing on the Tool of Unconditional Love with your own children? Are you doing with your kids what your dad did with you or what culture has taught you? Describe how that's going.

What, if anything, would you like to see change in how you're parenting them in regard to communicating covenant love?

A father paints a picture of God in the minds of his children. But if Dad is painting with an angry brush or a selfish brush or an uncaring brush, what picture of God is he producing? This isn't about bashing your father—it's about understanding yourself. On this topic of unconditional love, what kind of brush are you using and what kind of picture of God are you painting for your kids?

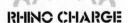

RHINO CHARGE

Fighting for the hearts of your children

Use the space below these Scripture references to record what the Lord shows you.

Genesis 15:12–20 (Covenant with Abram)

Deuteronomy 29 (Covenant renewal)

Galatians 3:13–20

Romans 8:38–39

2 Corinthians 1:22

Ephesians 4:30

Romans 11:6

Hebrews 10:14

Acts 2:38–39

A WORD FROM COACH KENNY

I remember the first time I heard Tim describe the difference between covenant love and consumer love—it took my breath away. I'm a high school football coach. I live in a world of constant competition, striving for improvement, pushing for numbers in the weight room, and having a scoreboard always declaring who won or lost every contest. We joke in my profession that you are only as good as your last game. It is all about performance, winning, and "What have you done for me lately?"

If I am not careful, I can easily take this mentality into my parenting. Of course, in my heart, I know that I love my children *no matter what.* I know that my love is not dependent on their performance. But do *they* know that?

> And I am convinced that nothing can ever separate us from God's love. Neither death nor life, neither angels nor demons, neither our fears for today nor our worries about tomorrow—not even the powers of hell can separate us from God's love. No power in the sky above or in the earth below—indeed, nothing in all creation will ever be able to separate us from the love of God that is revealed in Christ Jesus our Lord. (Rom. 8:38–39 NLT)

Rhino dad, you hold the paintbrush *today* that can paint a picture that will allow your child to understand the truth of this scripture. Can you imagine the confidence, trust, and security your children could experience if they had *no doubt* about the fact that there was *nothing* that could separate them from your love? What if they knew for a fact that there was *nothing* they could do to make you love them more or less?

I believe with all my heart that as our kids experience that our love is the covenant kind and not the consumer kind, they will be empowered to love in the same way. Rhino dad, ignite a *revolution* inside your own family by using the Tool of Unconditional Love.

M46 MOMENT

Todd

During my son Zack's sophomore year in high school, I started attending the M46 meetings led by Coach Dallas and Tim Sexton. At every session, we received a challenge to do with our kids. At one particular meeting, they challenged us to sit down at the dinner table and ask our sons and daughters this question: "Do you think there is anything you could do that would make me love you more or less?" They told us to ask the question and then just sit and listen, keep our mouths shut, let the kids speak, take it in, and, if necessary, ask for forgiveness.

I accepted the challenge. I'd been coaching Zack in football for years and I thought I'd been doing great by spending so much time with him and pulling for his success. So I figured I'd be safe. But after asking the question, Zack *blasted* me. Or at least that's the way it felt in the moment.

"Dad," Zack said, "you wore me out. You wore me out *at home* about football, on the way *to* football, and then *at* football practice! Then you wore me out all the way home *from* football! You never stopped! It never ended. Nothing was ever good enough! You made me play against guys two years older than me. You always made me hit the hardest players on the team."

Then my teenage son delivered his very loud knockout punch: "Dad, I … hated … football! Absolutely hated it!"

The entire time, I was trying to hold back the tears. Of course, as a dad who deeply loves his son, I would never mean to do anything to hurt him. But that day, I realized I *had* been hurting him, unknowingly, his entire life. I'd started coaching Zack when he was three years old, and when we had that conversation, he was sixteen. That's a lot of years to hate something you're doing.

Finally, I couldn't hold back the tears any longer. "Zack," I pleaded, "please forgive me! I am so sorry!"

My son responded, "I already forgave you. But also, Dad, if it wasn't for you and what you did, I wouldn't be the man I am today."

In that very tough moment of truth, my relationship with my son was restored. But here's the kicker: I hadn't realized our relationship was broken. This terrible wound remained invisible until I asked the question from the M46 Dads challenge.

How long would Zack have gone without telling me the truth? Would he ever have? How long would I have gone on not knowing? The great news is that it doesn't matter anymore, because I did ask and he answered with honesty. While the truth hurts, it can also set us free.

My life was changed, as was the relationship between me and my son, all because I accepted the challenge to ask him one simple question.

I knew immediately I had to change my behavior so that it was about Zack and not about me. I stopped going to his practices. And after games, I just told him how awesome he played. Sometimes he would say, "Don't lie, Dad. You know I stunk it up out there." And we would just laugh. Because we had been set free to focus on our relationship.

It turned out that my son went far past my expectations in playing football, and he played because he wanted to. He was a three-year starter, winning three state championships in a row. He had a couple of offers to play football in college but declined. I firmly believe that if I had not asked that challenge question, he would have continued playing football just to please me. That M46 challenge allowed me to understand the pressure I had put on my son for way too many years and how that had made him feel.

Today, Zack and I have intimate conversations where you can feel the love we have for each other. He is now able to talk to me and express *anything*. Praise God!

Zack

Growing up, my dad made sure of two things. First, that I served God. He made sure I served Him by always setting a godly example, taking our family to church, and spending time in the Word to discern how to lead us.

And second, that I played football. He was always my coach. Some people think having your dad as the coach would be an easy thing to deal with. But from the son's perspective, this can be one of the most challenging things to grow up with. I was always treated differently than the rest of my teammates, and the expectations on me were higher than on anyone else.

My dad and I always had the best relationship—except when it came time to call him "coach." How can any athlete perform at his maximum ability with the insane amount of pressure of always wanting to satisfy his dad?

But everything changed my sophomore year of high school. M46 Dads launched, and my father went to CRASHes every time the doors were open. As he continued to go to the meetings, the opportunity opened up for us to talk and really be honest. Because of one specific conversation, for the first time, I was able to play the game I loved with zero anxiety and without me stressing over how well I played.

My dad began to see the game from a different perspective and was able to cheer me on without any instruction or finding fault. Where he used to fight for *perfection*, he began fighting for *love*. He let me know that as long as I loved what I was doing, he was content. He began to see that my desires are not always his desires.

That change made the pressure fall off my shoulders like links from a chain. He developed a love for just being a fan and that allowed me to excel. Through this, our relationship grew closer. I was able to come to my dad in situations where before I would never have been able to confide in him. M46 Dads didn't just change my dad's life, but mine too.

THE CHALLENGE: FIGHT FOR THEIR HEARTS!

"In the future, when your children ask you,
'What do these stones mean?' tell them."

Joshua 4:6–7a (NIV)

Document your challenge here. The more detailed you are, the more you will be able to look back and tell your children the story of God's faithfulness in your life.

Rhino dad, you are the most influential man in your child's life. This chapter was about God's incredible proactive love for His people, and how as dads we get to communicate and demonstrate that love to our children.

Write down a list of three relationships in your life that you would consider consumer relationships:

1.

2.

3.

Write down three relationships in your life that you would consider covenant relationships:

1.

2.

3.

What kind of love do you think you have communicated and demonstrated to your kids?

Make an appointment with your kids, one at a time. Explain to them that God's love for His children is not based on their performance, but on the performance of His Son. Jesus lived the perfect life that God requires. At salvation, Jesus gives us His perfect performance in exchange for our failures.

Explain to your children that you love them with a covenant love. Tell them that there is nothing they could do that would make you love them more and nothing they could do that would make you love them less.

This is one of those catalyst moments, rhino dad. Give them an example of a time when you suspect you may have communicated a consumer love for them. Maybe it was when they brought home a grade that didn't meet your standards. Maybe there was a time when you were particularly disappointed in their behavior. Maybe there were times when you have communicated impatience with them. Give them one or more examples of when you didn't love them exactly like God loves His children.

Acknowledging your inability to love perfectly can be an incredibly powerful gift. You're not God. You are imperfect. He is perfect. Let your kids know that you are following Him and you want to love them like He loves us. Apologize if an apology is needed. Be specific. This challenge is all about you pointing your kids toward the covenant love of God and reminding them that you, despite your failures, are doing your best to model that same love for them.

Remember, rhino dad, this is all about showing them that God truly does love them unconditionally and that their standing before God is based on Jesus alone.

CRASH 3

THE TEMPLE

Dear rhino dad, have these pages open during the CRASH.

PRE-CRASH PREPARATION

Today's CRASH will equip you with the Tool of Transformation. To get the most out of today's CRASH:

> 1. Before you get to the meeting place, or as you're waiting for the CRASH to begin, flip back through the previous pages. Remind yourself what we talked about, reread what notes you wrote, and refresh your mind about how the challenge went.
>
> 2. If possible, silence your phone and put it away. Focus your full attention on being equipped to be the dad your children deserve.
>
> 3. Make sure you are fully present by saying a short prayer simply asking the Lord to clear your mind and give you "ears to hear" what you need today to prepare you to lead your family.
>
> 4. Be open and transparent with other men at your CRASH. Receive the help you need from another dad and/or provide encouragement to another dad as you both walk this fatherhood journey.

REVIEW AND TABLE TIME

Write down some of the main points from last session's review.

What came up in the discussion that you'd like to commit to pray about? Anything you can do to encourage one of the men at your table?

VIDEO NOTES

As you watch today's video, write down the main points.

IMAGE

The following image is provided to help you remember the main principle of this session and also to help you reteach this to your children or friends.

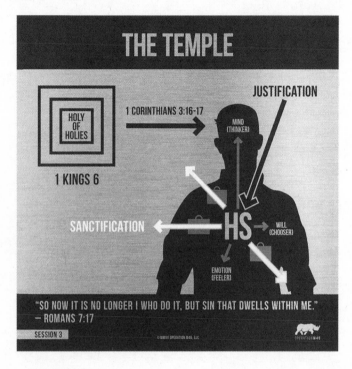

KEY SCRIPTURE

"Therefore, as one trespass led to condemnation for all men, so one act of righteousness leads to justification and life for all men. For as by the one man's disobedience the many were made sinners, so by the one man's obedience the many will be made righteous."
Romans 5:18–19

Paraphrase the passage in your own words.

THE TOOL

Each CRASH, we're putting a new tool in your hands. A tool is a principle that can guide your parenting.

In the third session, you have been handed the Tool of Transformation. In this session, we want to help you understand from God's Word exactly what happened to you when you became a child of God through salvation.

The goal is to help you communicate to your saved children exactly what happened to them when they were redeemed. They need to know that their standing before God is not based on their behavior but on their new birth. Ultimately, they need to know that if they are in Christ, they are holy, perfect, and blameless in His eyes, even on their worst day. And once they have been *justified* (made right with God), He will begin to *sanctify* (transform) them from the inside out.

Your kids need to know that God is working in them, and that the Christian life is about progress, not perfection. If they don't understand this truth, there's a good chance they will either become disillusioned and walk away or simply pursue "religion" and have an unhealthy fear of God for the rest of their lives.

THE CHALLENGE

Rhino dad, you are the most influential man in your child's life. This session was about the incredibly comprehensive nature of Jesus' finished work. The challenge is to allow your kids to see the process at work in you and to help them understand the process at work in them.

CRASH COURSE 3

Dear rhino dad, use the following pages to help you dig deeper into this session and record the challenge as you fight for the hearts of your children. Go through them at your own pace or just pick and choose which to do.

"If people really see that Christ has removed the fear of punishment from them by taking it into Himself, they won't do whatever they want, they'll do whatever He wants."

John Bunyan

THE HEART OF A RHINO

Hiroo Onoda was a Japanese intelligence officer in World War II. He was stationed on the island of Lubang in the Philippines in December 1944. His orders were to sabotage the harbor and the airfields to disrupt the impending American invasion. Onoda was trained in guerrilla warfare and believed that his emperor was a deity. His mother had given him a sword before the war to use to kill himself if he was ever about to be captured.

When the Americans invaded the Philippines in February 1945, Onoda and three other Japanese soldiers escaped into the jungle and refused to surrender. They pilfered rice patties and killed local cows for food. It is believed that Onoda killed about thirty people over the years, people he believed were enemy combatants.

In 1950, one of the other soldiers surrendered. The other two were killed in skirmishes with police in 1954 and 1972. Still, Onoda refused to surrender. Flyers were dropped into the jungle explaining that the war was over, but he believed they were enemy propaganda. Though he was declared officially dead in 1959, he considered himself to still be at war and was awaiting orders from his superiors.

In 1974, a Japanese student, Norio Suzuki, went to Lubang to try to find Onoda. He eventually did so and pleaded with him to return home. Onoda refused. Suzuki returned to Japan with an incredible story and some photographs. The Japanese eventually sent a delegation along with Onoda's brother and his former commander to plead with him to surrender and come home.

Onoda walked out of the jungle in 1974 in his tattered blue officer's uniform. He wept uncontrollably as he finally handed over his still-functioning rifle and sword. It was nearly thirty years after the war had ended. The Philippine president agreed to pardon him for those he had killed.

Hiroo Onoda had spent his life fighting a war that had already been decided. He never believed anyone who told him the war was over. He never believed any of the flyers that had been dropped to be real. All those years spent in the jungle, battling the elements and struggling for his life, fighting people who weren't even trying to kill him.

Rhino dad, do you believe that God is still angry with you? Are you fighting a war that's been over for a long time? Do you truly recognize that you're at peace with God because of the finished work of His Son? Do you have anxiety and fear associated with your standing before God?

Do your children who belong to God know that they have been made right forever, and that nothing can change that reality?

DIGGING DEEPER

In a couple of sentences, describe your own salvation experience. Were you an adult or a child when you were saved?

What do you make of Paul's teaching about you being "the righteousness of God in Him"? What does that mean?

What has the process of sanctification looked like in your life up to this point? What are some of the obstacles or baggage that God has been working through?

Rhino dad, your children need to know, especially as they grow older, where they stand with God. They will fail. They will struggle with sinful behaviors and flesh patterns. If they believe God is angry with them or is distancing Himself from them, they may become disillusioned and cynical about Christianity altogether. And they'll never experience intimacy with God. (That doesn't mean they're not responsible for their sin, however.)

One last thing: guilt, shame, and fear are the worst motivators. The fuel your kids will need to follow Jesus in this crazy world is knowing deep down in their DNA that they are already clean and totally acceptable to God right where they are, because Jesus is totally acceptable to God, and they are "hidden in Christ" (see Col. 3:3). This is the good news of the gospel!

RHINO COLLISION
Examining your own heart

LEARNED FROM MY DAD

Dads are teaching their children how to live, but they are also "painting a picture of God" with their daily actions. The same is true in your relationship with your own dad.

As we think about the Tool of Transformation, let's take a look at what your father taught you. Ask yourself the following questions and be brutally honest.

This isn't about bashing your father. He did the best he could with what *he* had been given. This is about calling things what they are and assessing the toolbox we walked into fatherhood carrying.

Why do you think it is so difficult to grasp that as children of God we are holy, perfect, and blameless in the eyes of God?

Do you think your children (if they are born again) understand that they are the temple of God? What difference do you think it might make in their lives if they understood it?

This is a tough question, but do you think you may have deposited some negative baggage in the lives of your children? We challenge you to own it, talk to your kids about it, and ask for forgiveness.

How would you explain to your children that our righteousness in Christ never gives us a license to sin?

LEARNED FROM MY CULTURE

Colossians 2:8 (NIV) commands us, "See to it that no one takes you captive through hollow and deceptive philosophy, which depends on human tradition and the elemental spiritual forces of this world rather than on Christ."

We are shaped not only by what we were taught by our father but also by our culture. Ask yourself the following questions and be brutally honest.

What do we learn about religion from our secular culture (Hollywood, TV, music, etc.)?

Why do you think so many people believe that in order to go to heaven when you die you have to be a good person?

How does the knowledge that we are free from condemnation actually motivate a person to live for God's glory?

What messages have you received from the church or from Christians about the gospel, how God looks at you, and what His expectations are of you?

A WORD FROM PASTOR TIM

What is it that makes you acceptable to God? Is God angry with you when you fail to live up to His standard of perfection? How can the Bible say that you are "the righteousness of God" (2 Cor. 5:21) even in the middle of your struggles with sin? Maybe you don't seem to be "growing" at the same pace as other men you know. Why? If you are a Christian, why do you think, choose, and feel the sinful things you do? Why does there seem to be a tension between what is taught in the Old Testament and the New Testament?

These are just some of the questions that many Christians wrestle with. And even if a person can *intellectually* accede to what the Bible says about these things, *experientially* it might be a different story. We are either right with God or we're not. And your answer to that biggest-of-all questions will profoundly impact your relationship with God, how you interact with Him, understand Him, talk about Him, *and share Him with your children.*

Clearly, if His standard for our acceptance is perfection, we're all in trouble … unless He does something about that problem for us. And therein lies the gospel. He did do something about that problem for us. In fact, He has done every single thing that needs to be done to make us forever right with Him. That sounds scandalous … because it is. But it's still true!

But, rhino dad, here's the thing: our standing before God has been resolved. It's not *being* resolved. It has been resolved. Our kids need to know whether they are still objects of God's wrath or His deeply loved children. There is no in-between. They have to experientially know it!

You, as a dad, get to be used by God to convince your children who belong to Him that all of those haunting questions have been answered by the finished work of Jesus. You get to help them see that this reality does not give us a right to go live however we please. It is the motivation to surrender their entire lives to Jesus.

My pastor once said, "Jesus didn't just die *for* you, He died *as* you." What an incredible thing to consider. What a life-changing place to live from!

REWRITING YOUR STORY

Regardless of what your father gave you and what your culture has handed to you, you can be a cycle breaker for good. It's time to be *intentional* about what you will pass down to your children.

Do you think your dad taught you to fear or love God?

How can you be proactive in helping your children understand the truly good news of the gospel?

RHINO CHARGE
Fighting for the hearts of your children

Use the space below these Scripture references to record what the Lord shows you.

1 Corinthians 3:16–17

2 Corinthians 6:14–18

Ephesians 2:19–22

1 Peter 2:5

Ephesians 1:13

Galatians 2:20

Hebrews 2:11

Hebrews 10:10

Hebrews 10:14

Hebrews 13:12

1 Corinthians 6:11

Philippians 1:6

Romans 5–6

A WORD FROM COACH KENNY

I don't know if you were like me, but when I was saved and started following the Lord, I knew God's Spirit was inside of me because there truly was a desire to honor and follow Him as I'd never had.

But at the same time, I was confused. I was confused because I still had some of the same temptations I'd had before I was saved. I was tempted to use words I knew I shouldn't, look at images I knew I shouldn't, and react in ways I knew I shouldn't.

I remember thinking, *What is wrong with me?* I truly wanted to follow the Lord, but I was still "prone to wander." It was like there was now a civil war inside of me, and I did not understand what was going on.

To be completely honest, going to church didn't always make it better. In fact, many times, it made it worse. At church, it seemed like everybody had it all together. The thought of speaking up and asking who else had my same struggles and temptations didn't exactly feel comfortable. So, I just kept the civil war to myself.

Tim refers to this session and the Tool of Transformation as game changers, and I could not agree more. That is exactly what they were for me. For years, I had heard that we all had something called a "flesh." But it wasn't until I began to understand that flesh is made up of our thinker (brain), our feeler (heart), and our chooser (will) that it all started to make sense.

I learned that as we go about our lives, our flesh picks up baggage that fuels the temptations we have and drives the bad decisions we make. But Scripture says our bodies are a temple of God's Spirit (1 Cor. 6:19–20). If we have surrendered ourselves to follow the Lord, we now have God's Spirit inside us.

I understood all that. The part I didn't understand was that, even though God's Spirit was now in me, I still had a thinker, feeler, and chooser that had baggage that had to be dealt with. I now understood why there was a civil war inside of me.

As a parent, this has helped me so many times. One day, one of my sons came to me, and I could see on his face that he was absolutely broken. He could barely look me in the eye, but through tears he told me that he had been looking at things on a device that he knew he shouldn't. I remember the shame, guilt, and fear on his face as he asked me, "What's wrong with me? Why would I look at stuff like that when I know it's wrong? Maybe I am not a Christian."

In that moment, I was able to explain to him why we have a civil war inside us. I told him that I, too, have to deal with the exact same temptation he does. When I told him that, his face literally lit up in amazement but also relief. I told him we would walk through it together.

As we sat there together, we discussed the civil war between the spirit and flesh that every man has … and we discussed a way that we could help each other deal with this temptation. I truly believe, in that moment, my relationship with my son changed forever. It truly was a game changer.

M46 MOMENT

One day, I met a young man named Brent who showed up at my (Tim's) office, truly at the end of himself. He had lost everything. He'd spent the previous month living in Savannah, Georgia, trying to drink his problems away. His fiancée, with whom he shared three children, was done with him, and she had good reason. "I was a completely angry person," Brent told me. "My mom would talk to me about anything, and I'd just get mad at her. My fiancée would talk to me about anything; I'd just get mad at her. It was always just anger, anger, anger." One morning when he woke up, his first thought was, *There has to be more to life than this.*

Brent and I began to meet once or twice a week. His concept of God and his understanding of the gospel were pretty typical for someone who grew up in the Bible Belt but wasn't a believer. The difference was that now he was ready to listen—and he had a thousand questions. We talked a lot about what the gospel is and what it isn't. God worked on his heart and dispelled many myths around who He is and what Jesus has done.

I didn't try to lead Brent in a "sinner's prayer." I've met with lots of men in my office who are hurting and want God to make it stop. And I have noticed over the years that, sometimes, hurting people will see the sinner's prayer as a sort of contract negotiation with God. I didn't want that for him. Anyway, something was different about Brent's attitude. He knew he needed Jesus, whether He made his problems go away or not.

One day at home, all on his own, Brent prayed, and Jesus saved him. "I just see everything in a different light," he said later. "The love for my kids, the love for my fiancée, the love for my mom, the love for a lot of people. It's just overwhelming."

Admittedly, in situations like this, I struggle with skepticism. I watch young guys like Brent come out of chaos and a party lifestyle, and I sometimes wonder how long their newfound faith will last. I've seen guys walk away from God when He doesn't "perform" as they want Him to or instantly mend all the messes they have made. Maybe they never got saved in the first place. Or maybe their wandering is a necessary part of their process of "working out their salvation."

But as I baptized Brent in the Easter season of 2020, and as I've watched him grow, it has been incredibly encouraging to me. I have no idea if Brent's family will ever be together again. Brent is not demanding that of God. He's humbly walking with his new King. And I do know that God is transforming his life. He's loving his children from a brand-new place. His mother, who is a believer, is so excited by what she sees Jesus doing in her son's life. Brent even led his nephew to Christ.

Brent is a work in progress, just like the rest of us. There is baggage in his life that God is revealing to him and freeing him from. He acknowledges now what his flesh patterns are and how those patterns have affected the people in his life. Brent has learned to confess his failures specifically and not deny them. He has even apologized to his children for the man he was before. In many ways, he has become an inspiration to me, and a confirmation that God changes lives when people throw up their hands in surrender to Him.

I know that God is faithful and just in completing what He has begun in Brent's life. And his children will get a front-row seat to the transforming power of the gospel.

THE CHALLENGE: FIGHT FOR THEIR HEARTS!

"In the future, when your children ask you,
'What do these stones mean?' tell them."

Joshua 4:6–7a (NIV)

Document your challenge here. The more detailed you are, the more you will be able to look back and tell your children the story of God's faithfulness in your life.

Rhino dad, you are the most influential man in your child's life.

Make an appointment with your kids, one at a time. Explain to them that God is not shocked or disappointed that they are not a finished product yet. Jesus came and died to make us right with God and to begin a process of making us more like Him.

Tell them about your salvation experience. When and how did you get saved? (The exact date is not important.)

Tell them about some of the baggage in your life that has made it sometimes difficult to hear and believe that you are holy, perfect, and blameless in Christ. Be honest about your own struggles.

Talk to them about their own assurance that they belong to God. Ask them about the baggage that makes it difficult for them to a) believe that the gospel is true and b) obey God.

Rhino dad, we know you want your kids to have a shot at a real, intimate relationship with Jesus. Help them see that there are no obstacles (if they have been born again) between them and God. You get to help them understand that God rejoices in our *progress* and is not angry with us all over again when we stumble.

The Bible is full of passages that talk about the battle between our flesh and God's Spirit in us. In Galatians 5:16–18, for example, Paul was trying to convince people who were being burdened with the requirements of the law (external behavior) to trust in what had been accomplished internally through the gospel.

Rhino dad, the gospel is a person. His name is Jesus. God had wrath because of our failures and sins, and Jesus took it on Himself at the cross. Before that, He lived the perfect life that we can't live.

If your son or your daughter is born again, then he or she has been given Jesus' perfection. Do they know that? Do they believe that? Remember, they won't always act like that's true, and they won't necessarily feel like it's true. But as dads, we get to communicate this gospel reality to our children.

CRASH 4

L.A.W.S.

Dear rhino dad, have these pages open during the CRASH.

PRE-CRASH PREPARATION

Today's CRASH will equip you with the Tool of Emotional Needs.
To get the most out of today's CRASH:

1. Before you get to the meeting place, or as you're waiting for the CRASH to begin, flip back through the previous pages. Remind yourself what we talked about, reread what notes you wrote, and refresh your mind about how the challenge went.

2. If possible, silence your phone and put it away. Focus your full attention on being equipped to be the dad your children deserve.

3. Make sure you are fully present by saying a short prayer simply asking the Lord to clear your mind and give you "ears to hear" what you need today to prepare you to lead your family.

4. Be open and transparent with other men at your CRASH. Receive the help you need from another dad and/or provide encouragement to another dad as you both walk this fatherhood journey.

REVIEW AND TABLE TIME

Write down some of the main points from last session's review.

What came up in the discussion that you'd like to commit to pray about? Anything you can do to encourage one of the men at your table?

VIDEO NOTES

As you watch today's video, write down the main points.

IMAGE

The following image is provided to help you remember the main principle of this session and also to help you reteach this to your children or friends.

KEY SCRIPTURE

"And my God will supply every need of yours according to his riches in glory in Christ Jesus."
Philippians 4:19

Paraphrase the passage in your own words.

THE TOOL

Each CRASH, we're putting a new tool in your hands. A tool is a principle that can guide your parenting.

In the fourth session, you have been handed the Tool of Emotional Needs. We were all created with four basic needs. In the video, we use the acronym L.A.W.S. to describe these needs, which are love, acceptance, worth, and security.

We were meant to find these needs met in our relationship with Christ. But we all develop what we call "flesh patterns," consistent ways we try to get those needs met apart from God. That's our definition of sin: you and me trying to get our needs met apart from God.

Learn to acknowledge your own flesh patterns. Acknowledge the ways you have tried to get your needs of love, acceptance, worth, and security met apart from God. You need to see these for yourself. And our ultimate goal is that your children would recognize that they have these same needs, and that God wants them to find those needs met in Him. Help your kids see the flesh patterns that have developed in their lives, the ways that they tend to try to find those needs met apart from God.

THE CHALLENGE

Dad, you are the most influential man in your child's life. This is the one session that probably had the most profound impact on the day-to-day life of my (Tim's) boys. If you really want to help your children walk in the freedom that the gospel provides, then you have to help them understand the real, practical implications of the gospel.

This is one of those things that can help your children recognize and experience the difference between pursuing religion simply because that's what good Christian folks do, and experiencing the life-changing force that is the gospel. Once your children see this at work in their own lives, they'll never be the same

CRASH COURSE 4

Dear rhino dad, use the following pages to help you dig deeper into this session and record the challenge as you fight for the hearts of your children. Go through them at your own pace or just pick and choose which to do.

> *"It does not matter what your personal deficiency, or whether it be a hundred and one different things, God has always one sufficient answer, His Son Jesus Christ, and He is the answer to every need."*
>
> Watchman Nee

THE HEART OF A RHINO

History is strewn with stories of people who have tried to find their needs met by what this world has to offer ... and come up wanting.

One place we see this played out is in the strange world of celebrity. It has been said that many entertainers are drawn to that world because they need validation, affirmation, acceptance, or applause. A March 2014 article in *Psychology Today* said that fame is like a drug.[4] The article noted that when fame begins to slip away from the once-famous, they may begin to come apart. The need for the acceptance of others can be as powerful as any drug.

In 1970, a young woman decided to attend the ten-year high school reunion for the Thomas Jefferson High School (Port Arthur, Texas) class of 1960. She had felt like an outsider when she was in school. When asked if she had attended her senior prom, she answered, "Nobody asked me." When asked if she had felt different from her classmates, she said, "I felt apart from them." After high school, she briefly attended the University of Texas at Austin. While there, some fraternities voted her "ugliest man on campus." It bothered her deeply for the rest of her life.

She appeared on *The Dick Cavett Show* on June 25, 1970. They began to talk about her upcoming high school reunion. Cavett asked her, "Were you surrounded by friends in high school?" She answered, "They laughed me out of class, out of town, out of the state, man." Then she said, "So, I'm going home."

On October 4, 1970, just a few months after her reunion, she was found dead on the floor in her hotel room in Los Angeles. Janis Joplin had overdosed on heroin.

She joined the infamous 27-Club: Jimi Hendrix, Jim Morrison, Amy Winehouse, Kurt Cobain, among others, all dead at the age of twenty-seven. Many who knew Janis said she was looking for validation and acceptance her whole life.

Rhino dad, we don't want our sons and daughters walking through life hungry and thirsty for love, acceptance, worth, and security. If they don't know they are complete in this life, there is no telling where they might go, or what they might reach for, to find fulfillment.

DIGGING DEEPER

Remember, every human being ever created is born with the need for love, acceptance, worth, and security. These are needs, not just wants. All of us have to have L.A.W.S. We were created by God to find these basic needs met in Christ. If you are a child of God, then these needs are met already.

How do we know that in Christ we have all the love we will ever need (1 John 4:7–9)?

How do we know that we are fully accepted by God today, right where we are (Col. 1:21–22)?

How do we know how much we are worth to God (Rom. 5:8)?

How do we know that we are secure in our relationship with God and that He will never throw us away, no matter what (Eph. 1:13)?

Think about this, rhino dad: What amazing things might God do in the life of a man who knows he is complete in Christ and all his needs are met already? How would your sons' and daughters' lives be different if they grew up knowing that they are not in need of any more love, acceptance, worth, and security? How can you help them to understand they are complete even when they don't feel that way?

RHINO COLLISION
Examining your own heart

LEARNED FROM MY DAD

Dads are teaching their children how to live, but they are also "painting a picture of God" with their daily actions. The same is true in your relationship with your own dad.

As we think about the Tool of Emotional Needs, let's take a look at what your father taught you. Ask yourself the following questions and be brutally honest.

This isn't about bashing your father. He did the best he could with what *he* had been given. This is about calling things what they are and assessing the toolbox we walked into fatherhood carrying.

Thinking back to your father, what did you learn from your dad about your emotional needs?

Thinking back to your father, did he communicate well that you were loved and accepted? What did he express about how much you are worth to him? How well did he demonstrate that you were secure in his love for you?

LEARNED FROM MY CULTURE

Colossians 2:8 (NIV) commands us, "See to it that no one takes you captive through hollow and deceptive philosophy, which depends on human tradition and the elemental spiritual forces of this world rather than on Christ."

We are shaped not only by what we were taught by our father but also by our culture. Ask yourself the following questions and be brutally honest.

What does our culture say about what human beings need internally?

What does our culture teach us about where we are to find love?

How is love defined in our culture?

In our current culture, what is it that makes people "acceptable"? (Think about work, social settings, school, church, etc.)

What determines one's value and worth in our culture?

What does our culture say about where security is found?

What messages have you received about love, acceptance, worth, and security from the church or from Christians? How can the church help or hurt in this area?

A WORD FROM PASTOR TIM

I remember the day Scott Brittin at Grace Ministries International wrote the words *Love, Acceptance, Worth,* and *Security* on the whiteboard. I don't know if it was just me, or if everyone in the room felt the same, but everything came to a stop. I knew he was putting a finger on what had been driving me my whole life. The Holy Spirit did something in me that day that is difficult to describe.

From that moment forward, Paul's words from Galatians 5, where he talks about walking in the Spirit and no longer gratifying the desires of the flesh, came to life for me. I had been grasping to find my needs met on my own, apart from Christ, but I had never seen it that way.

Over the years, I have talked through this idea quite a bit with my own boys. It has transformed the way they see what's going on inside of them. They know that the Holy Spirit lives in them. They know that His Spirit in us is 100 percent obedient to God. They also know that their flesh is 100 percent rebellious toward God. They know that the Christian life isn't about improving their flesh or becoming a better version of themselves. They know that it's about learning to walk in the Spirit. It's about believing God when He says we are complete and in need of nothing.

Now when they are tempted to reach for something other than Jesus to meet these needs, they can see the difference between the desires of their flesh and the desires of the Spirit, and they can choose. They don't get to pretend they don't know the difference, and they don't get to say, "This is just the way I am." They can choose to walk in the Spirit and deny their flesh, because they recognize the difference.

REWRITING YOUR STORY

Regardless of what your father gave you and what your culture has handed to you, you can be a cycle breaker for good. It's time to be *intentional* about what you will pass down to your children.

Can you see yourself doing with your kids what your dad did with you, good or bad? Describe how that's going. How are you doing on this issue with your own children?

What, if anything, would you like to see change in how you're parenting them in terms of their L.A.W.S.?

RHINO CHARGE

Fighting for the hearts of your children

Use the space below these Scripture references to record what the Lord shows you.

Philippians 4:19

1 John 4:7–9

Colossians 1:21–22

Romans 5:8

Ephesians 1:13

John 4:7–10

A WORD FROM COACH KENNY

Our hope is that the tools you learn in these sessions aren't used only in your challenge. We hope they will be parenting principles you use for the rest of your life. It doesn't get much more practical than this session.

I remember hearing Tim teach this session for the first time. It filled in so many blanks for me. The fact that every one of us has certain emotional needs that we must have met—love, acceptance or adequacy, worth, and security—made so much sense to me.

I remember suddenly understanding, even as Tim was teaching this session, why people wore bell-bottomed pants back in the '70s and parachute pants with one glove in the '80s. I realized why, as a high school football coach, I had to battle the feeling that my worth was directly tied to my yearly win/loss record.

Seriously, if you really think about the truth of the Tool of Emotional Needs, you even begin to understand things like why young men join gangs and why young ladies can be so promiscuous with their bodies—they're all just looking for love, acceptance, worth, and security.

When I was in college, I had a teammate who badly wanted to be a part of a fraternity. But to be a part of this fraternity, you had to allow yourself to be branded. This was a process of heating up a metal rod and pressing it into the flesh to burn a symbol on the body. My teammate was terrified and wanted nothing to do with this, but he agreed to it anyway. I asked him why, and he said he really wanted to be accepted by that fraternity.

As we think about the Tool of Emotional Needs, we have to realize that every one of our needs can be met through understanding our true identity in Christ. This is true both for us and for our children. Our children have the same emotional needs we do, and if they don't find love, acceptance, worth, and security in their true identity in Christ, they are going to go out looking for them.

Country singer Johnny Lee laments in his famous song, "Lookin' for love in all the wrong places." Rhino dad, if your children don't understand the Tool of Emotional Needs, that is exactly what could happen to them.

All that said, I want you to imagine how powerful this tool can be in forming a deeper, more transparent relationship with your children. What if you were willing to share with them your own struggles as it relates to these needs? Imagine the difference in your child's life if they felt the freedom to discuss with you their deepest thoughts concerning their emotional needs. You now know they are going to get it from somewhere. Fight for their hearts!

M46 MOMENT

I (Tim) have four boys. It has been fascinating to watch this concept play out in my home over the last twenty-five or so years. I remember the first real "girlfriend" that one of our boys had. That kid was smitten. This particular son of ours wore his heart on his sleeve. He's a genuinely considerate and thoughtful guy, and I knew he might be the most vulnerable in relationships because of his generous nature. He was always so accommodating and respectful with this young lady. But Georgia and I were a little worried because this girl didn't ever seem to be quite as interested in him as he was in her.

I remember how every now and then he would ask me why it was so difficult for him to tell what she was thinking. I wanted to laugh and say, "Son, get in the boat with the rest of us." He would say things like, "Dad, sometimes when I see her, she acts like she's so excited to see me, and the next time I see her, it's like I'm invisible."

For several weeks, he was really concerned about how to get her attention. One day, I picked him up from some event, and when he hopped in the car, he said, "Dad, I learned something tonight. I realized that my whole day is either good or bad based on how she responds when I see her. So I'm out. I see that I'm trying to get something from her that I already have in Jesus. I don't think I need a girlfriend right now."

That was one of the best days of my life as a dad. That was a real M46 Moment for me. It might sound silly, but I knew right then and there that he got it! He noticed his own propensity to be an emotional beggar. Because of this, I think God rescued him from countless moments of heartache. He gracefully ended that relationship, by the way, and he's been keenly aware ever since that he has the tendency to try to find life itself in the acceptance of other people. He has grown spiritually, and part of that is due to his willingness to recognize his own flesh's attempts to find L.A.W.S. apart from Christ.

THE CHALLENGE: FIGHT FOR THEIR HEARTS!

"In the future, when your children ask you,
'What do these stones mean?' tell them."

Joshua 4:6–7a (NIV)

Document your challenge here. The more detailed you are, the more you will be able to look back and tell your children the story of God's faithfulness in your life.

Rhino dad, you are the most influential man in your child's life.

Set aside a specific time to begin this conversation with your kids, one at a time. And, dads, be prepared to be transparent with them. Think about the wrong ways you have tried to find love, acceptance, worth, or security. It shouldn't be that difficult. We all do it. Share some examples with them (age-appropriate, of course).

Rhino dad, in what ways have you tried to get one or more of these needs met apart from God? What have been some of the adverse consequences?

Why is it so difficult to believe that these needs are actually already met in Christ?

Ask your child about each one of these needs. How might he or she try to get these needs met apart from God? Does he or she struggle in any of these particular areas?

Love

Acceptance

Worth

Security

Let your children know that every single human being ever created has struggled trying to get these needs met. But as followers of Jesus, we get to acknowledge and confess our flesh patterns and actually begin to find freedom.

Ask your children this question: What would it be like to walk into your school, locker room, workplace—any environment—and know that you don't need anyone to like you, accept you, or think you're cool? What would it be like to be that free?

That's what the gospel provides: freedom! But remember, it's about progress, not perfection. Let your children know that you want to help them find real freedom in Christ.

THE FOUR RHINOS

Dear rhino dad, have these pages open during the CRASH.

PRE-CRASH PREPARATION

Today's CRASH will equip you with the Tool of Parenting Styles. To get the most out of today's CRASH:

1. Before you get to the meeting place, or as you're waiting for the CRASH to begin, flip back through the previous pages. Remind yourself what we talked about, reread what notes you wrote, and refresh your mind about how the challenge went.

2. If possible, silence your phone and put it away. Focus your full attention on being equipped to be the dad your children deserve.

3. Make sure you are fully present by saying a short prayer simply asking the Lord to clear your mind and give you "ears to hear" what you need today to prepare you to lead your family.

4. Be open and transparent with other men at your CRASH. Receive the help you need from another dad and/or provide encouragement to another dad as you both walk this fatherhood journey.

REVIEW AND TABLE TIME

Write down some of the main points from last session's review.

What came up in the discussion that you'd like to commit to pray about? Anything you can do to encourage one of the men at your table?

VIDEO NOTES

As you watch today's video, write down the main points.

IMAGE

The following image is provided to help you remember the main principle of this session and also to help you reteach this to your children or friends.

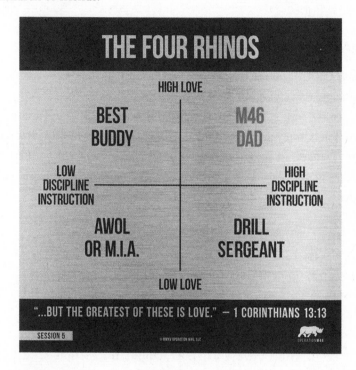

KEY SCRIPTURE

"Love the LORD your God with all your heart and with all your soul and with all your strength. These commandments that I give you today are to be on your hearts. Impress them on your children. Talk about them when you sit at home and when you walk along the road, when you lie down and when you get up."

Deuteronomy 6:5–7 (NIV)

Paraphrase the passage in your own words.

THE TOOL

Each CRASH, we're putting a new tool in your hands. A tool is a principle that can guide your parenting.

In the fifth session, you have been handed the Tool of Parenting Styles. It is important to know what sort of father each of your children perceives you to be ... because each style tends to produce different results in children. Using two criteria—Discipline/Instruction and Love—we can form four quadrants of parenting styles:

1. High Love + Low Discipline/Instruction = **Best Buddy**
2. Low Love + Low Discipline/Instruction = **AWOL (absent without leave)**
3. Low Love + High Discipline/Instruction = **Drill Sergeant**
4. High Love + High Discipline/Instruction = **M46 Dad**

THE CHALLENGE

Dad, you are the most influential man in your child's life. Your challenge is to take your kids through the Four Dads quadrant exercise.

CRASH COURSE 5

Dear rhino dad, use the following pages to help you dig deeper into this session and record the challenge as you fight for the hearts of your children. Go through them at your own pace or just pick and choose which to do.

> *"Don't worry that children never listen to you;*
> *worry that they are always watching you."*
> Robert Fulghum

THE HEART OF A RHINO

In the 1920s, Dr. Evan Kane, a surgeon, faced a difficult dilemma. Many of his patients could not receive the basic surgeries they desperately needed. At that time, only general anesthesia (i.e., putting patients to sleep during surgery) was used. For those with heart conditions and other impairments, this was considered too dangerous. Dr. Kane had a theory that local anesthesia (in which the patient would not have to be put completely under) could be used for minor surgeries. But no one had ever tried this approach.

Dr. Kane looked for a volunteer to experiment with local anesthesia on an actual surgery, but he could find no takers. So on February 15, 1921, the good doctor successfully performed an appendectomy ... on himself.[5]

Now *that*, my friend, is total commitment—he was 100 percent all in. Cutting your own incision, risking yourself, and braving the pain for the greater good.

But, rhino dad, very often that is exactly what we must do for the greater good of our families. In this chapter, I am going to ask you to perform some surgery on yourself.

DIGGING DEEPER

This session provides a powerful tool for you to examine your parenting style and to figure out how each of your children perceives you. According to research, each parenting style generally produces certain results. Let's take a deeper look …

1. Best Buddy Dad (upper left quadrant)

- This is the combination of high love and low discipline/instruction. Permissive parenting tends to produce children with very low self-esteem and feelings of inferiority. Though the parents express a lot of love, the lack of boundaries leaves their children with a high level of insecurity. The kids feel loved, but they are never sure of their limits.

2. AWOL Dad (lower left quadrant)

- This is the combination of low love and low discipline. These children tend to grow up with little to no lasting relationship with the parents. They are estranged because they feel forsaken. The parents' neglect may not necessarily be intentional—they simply may be in the midst of their own traumas and chaos (addiction, abusive situation, etc.). These children grow up with unbelievably deep emotional scars, and their only hope is to find Christ, be surrounded by godly role models, and get some good Christian counseling.

3. Drill Sergeant Dad (lower right quadrant)

- This is the combination of low love and high discipline/instruction. These parents raise children who are provoked to rebellion. The bar is always high and the "musts" are always abundant, so there's a strong sense of safety. But this kind of parent isn't just content to win the war—he has to win every battle too. Communication between parent and child takes the form of arguing and fighting, especially once the child is old enough to fight back. These children feel squeezed by their parents to the point that they cannot wait to leave home. Many times, they rebel.

4. M46 Dad (upper right quadrant)

- This is the best combination of love and discipline. This parent has clear boundaries but is very loving … compassionate but firm authority. The result is a child high in self-esteem and equipped with good coping skills. This produces a child who is well adjusted and who maintains a positive relationship with their parents as they get older.

This section is from an article from Focus on the Family titled "4 Parenting Styles and Effective Child Discipline" by Chip Ingram. The article refers to a seminar on parenting presented by Dr. Richard Meier at the Meier Clinic in Dallas, Texas.[6]

RHINO COLLISION
Examining your own heart

LEARNED FROM MY DAD

Dads are teaching their children how to live, but they are also "painting a picture of God" with their daily actions. The same is true in your relationship with your own dad.

As we think about the Tool of Parenting Styles, let's take a look at what your father taught you. Ask yourself the following questions and be brutally honest.

This isn't about bashing your father. He did the best he could with what *he* had been given. This is about calling things what they are and assessing the toolbox we walked into fatherhood carrying.

Thinking back to your father … where would you put him on the "love line"? Where would you put him on the "discipline/instruction line"?

What was your father's parenting style? Which of the four rhinos is your dad?

What do you think you learned from your dad because of his parenting style?

What did you not learn from your dad because of his parenting style?

LEARNED FROM MY CULTURE

Colossians 2:8 (NIV) commands us, "See to it that no one takes you captive through hollow and deceptive philosophy, which depends on human tradition and the elemental spiritual forces of this world rather than on Christ."

We are shaped not only by what we were taught by our father but also by our culture. Ask yourself the following questions and be brutally honest.

What does our culture say a man's parenting style should be? Is one style looked upon more favorably or less favorably?

What would you say are most of your friends' parenting styles? How does that affect you?

What messages, if any, have you received about the importance of the four parenting styles from the church or from Christians?

A WORD FROM PASTOR TIM

I imagine that most every dad, while reflecting on this session, would say that he could fall into any one of these four categories on any given day. We all have days where we do better than others. I'm sure I've been all four at some point over the years. But most of the time, we will land in one of these four quadrants.

It could very well be that you are modeling what was modeled for you. Or maybe you're a cycle breaker who has vowed to do things differently from how your own father did. Maybe you feel like you're winging it and learning as you go. One thing we have discovered over the years is that what we perceive that we are communicating to our children and what we are actually communicating to our children might be two different things.

Rhino dad, this isn't about how much you love your children. We're not challenging your heart for them. We know you would take a bullet for them. This is about how they receive the love you think you're communicating. It's about how they perceive their relationship with you.

So the real significance of this session's challenge lies in asking your children where they would place you. In the end, however, we have to remember that you are painting a picture of God for your children to see. So pride and hurt feelings simply have to take a back seat. Do you really want to know what your kids think and feel when they see you coming? God is so good, rhino dad. Sometimes we just have to slow down and listen.

I have talked to so many dads who demand excellence from their kids at all times in every endeavor. I have also talked to dads who are far more lax in their expectations and despise the idea of causing anxiety in the hearts of their kids by demanding performance. Each one of those dads could make a case, even from Scripture, that they are doing it the only way it ought to be done.

Keep in mind that it's possible to communicate things that are technically true about God while simultaneously communicating something about God's heart that's not true at all. The "street preacher" screaming at passersby that they are going to hell if they don't repent might be communicating something that is technically true, but his method communicates something about God that is not true at all.

What is your parenting style communicating to your kids about who God is and what He is like? Being a dad requires nuance and attentiveness. If we want to paint an accurate picture of who God is for our children, we have to pay attention to what we're doing.

I have four boys, and they really are all different. I've had to learn over the years, sometimes the hard way, to pay attention to how they each respond to me. Being an intentional dad who is fighting for the hearts of his children requires wisdom, attentiveness, and patience.

We want to challenge you to own the truth about how you have been operating until now. Pay close attention to how you handle your children's academic life, their participation in sports, their home life, all of it.

Again, we know you love your kids. So allow God to hold that mirror up in front of your face. He loves you deeply, and He loves your children even more than you do. Let Him work. Allow Him to change you if He needs to change you. Make sure your children know you want to hear the truth, and be sure to receive what your kids say to you in response to this challenge. Don't get defensive. Your children will see Jesus in your humility.

REWRITING YOUR STORY

Regardless of what your father gave you and what your culture has handed to you, you can be a cycle breaker for good. It's time to be *intentional* about what you will pass down to your children.

How are you doing on the Tool of Parenting Styles with your own children? Are you simply doing with your kids what your dad did with you or what culture has taught you? Describe how that's going.

What, if anything, would you like to see change in the sort of dad you're being with them?

RHINO CHARGE
Fighting for the hearts of your children

Use the space below these Scripture references to record what the Lord shows you.

1 Corinthians 13:1–13

Deuteronomy 6:5–9

Ephesians 6:4

Hebrews 12:5–11

A WORD FROM COACH KENNY

Years ago, when I first did this challenge with my six kids, something happened that I never expected. After drawing out the quadrants and explaining the lines that form the graph, each of my kids gave me their feedback as to where I fit. It was eye-opening to realize that every one of them saw me in a slightly different way. But, for the most part, I was feeling pretty good.

Right up until one of them said, "But, Dad, can we be honest with you about Saturdays?" Saturday was the day each week that we took a chunk of time to clean around and outside the house. Having six kids (five being boys), you can imagine that, by the end of the week, everything needs to be cleaned up. The kids asked if they could show me where they would place me on the graph for every Saturday.

All six of them placed me in the "High Discipline/Instruction and Low Love" quadrant—the Drill Sergeant Dad!

They shared that they hated our Saturdays because I did nothing but bark orders, push everyone to work fast, and demand perfection with every small task and detail. They said, "Dad, it's like every Saturday morning you're running a football practice."

Have you ever heard the statement "People don't care how much you know until they know how much you care"? I have heard that my entire life and always tried to apply it with the people I work with. But it is true in our homes and families as well!

First Corinthians 13:13 (NIV) says, "And now these three remain: faith, hope and love. But the greatest of these is love." Isn't it interesting that God clearly declares love as greater than faith and hope? I mean, isn't faith the thing we have to have in order to be saved to have eternal life? And isn't hope so important that, if people are without hope, they begin to consider taking their own lives? Yet God is clearly saying that love is more powerful than both of these! Maybe that is why Paul boldly declares:

> If I speak in the tongues of men and of angels, but have not love, I am a noisy gong or a clanging cymbal. And if I have prophetic powers, and understand all mysteries and all knowledge, and if I have all faith, so as to remove mountains, but have not love, I am nothing. (1 Cor. 13:1–2)

Rhino dad, we can have the greatest advice, greatest instruction, greatest plans in the world to pass along to our kids … but if they don't truly know and feel that we love them, we can quickly become a "noisy gong" and lose our influence with them.

It is time for you to fight for the hearts of your children by finding out how they perceive your parenting style. This simple challenge could completely change the relationship you have with your children. Be intentional, and encourage them to be honest with you. Listen, and see what the Lord will show you.

This could change everything.

M46 MOMENT

The following M46 Moment comes from one of our dads in our CRASH Communities.

I have been blessed to be a part of M46 Dads since the beginning. The lessons I have learned during our sessions have helped improve my relationship with my four kids and my beautiful wife.

When I was eight, my own dad left with no notice and never came back. My mom later remarried, but my stepdad was never involved in our lives. The only thing I remember about him was one time at the dinner table when he got upset because I didn't eat my green beans. He proceeded to tell me how my life would not amount to "three cents" and I would *never* succeed.

That story sums up how I was raised. Not eating green beans meant my life would be worthless.

Ironically, though, that became a defining moment for me. I decided I would prove to my stepdad that I *could* succeed and that I *would* succeed.

That drive gave me some help in life, but it also came to have a profoundly negative effect on my relationship with my own kids.

I focused all my energy into my career rather than my family. I worked relentlessly to bring in enough wealth to prove that I was worth more than three cents. Unknowingly, my plan backfired, because I was giving my family only three cents' worth of love and attention.

When M46 Dads began, I worked every challenge with my own kids. I was learning how to build an intentional relationship with them. Before, my focus had always been work. Now, when I was with my family, I concentrated on making sure they knew I was focused on them. At least, I thought that was the case.

When I did the Four Dads challenge with them, I just knew it was going to be an easy discussion because of how involved I'd been in their lives. I was excited about all the things I was going to hear about what a great dad I was. After dinner that night, I plotted out the graph and explained the quadrants to my four kids. Then I had each of them do their own and place me on the graph.

I knew for three of my kids I would likely be somewhere in the Drill Sergeant zone. But for one son, I just knew the results would definitely be an M46 Dad. For the past six months, I had been coaching him in football. We spent three days a week talking during our car rides to and from practice. Sometimes we'd have to travel for a game, so he and I would spend six to eight hours together each Saturday. He and I were racking up a lot of time.

As my kids finished their graphs, I noticed he did not want me to see his result. Finally, he leaned into his mother and began to cry. I asked him what was wrong, and he said he didn't want to share what he had put on his paper. I explained again that whatever he drew would not matter and was going to help me grow as a father. Once again, I was thinking there was no way I was not the perfect dad in his eyes. Maybe the joy of him telling me was making him cry? But I was so wrong.

When he finally surrendered his graph, I saw he had labeled me as an AWOL Dad.

I launched into defense mode, breaking my assurance that whatever he said wouldn't bother me. But I quickly stopped because I saw how much he was hurting. He proceeded to tell me that for the past six months I had been there for sure but that I had never taken the time to ask what *he* wanted to talk about. I just *always* talked about football.

In that tough moment, I learned that being a part of my kids' lives is always more than just being there physically. I had to learn to serve my kids by *really* listening to them, by truly being present.

THE CHALLENGE: FIGHT FOR THEIR HEARTS!

"In the future, when your children ask you,
'What do these stones mean?' tell them."

Joshua 4:6–7a (NIV)

Document your challenge here. The more detailed you are, the more you will be able to look back and tell your children the story of God's faithfulness in your life.

Rhino dad, you are the most influential man in your child's life. Your challenge in this chapter is to take your kids through the Four Dads quadrant exercise. Follow the detailed instructions we have offered you here.

Pray before you engage with your children and ask for God's leadership and blessing over this crucial time for your family.

- Draw out the Four Rhinos graph on a piece of paper for each child.
- Explain to them very simply what each term means.
- Explain to them what the lines represent.
- Assure them there will be no consequences for their honesty with you (and be ready to honor that assurance, even if they tell you the worst thing you can imagine).
- Be certain they understand how to use the graph.
- Leave them alone for a few minutes to mark the graph.

- When they are done, thank them and reassure
  them.

When you get to see your kids' graphs, consider prayerfully how you might change the attitudes or actions that have caused your kids to rank you in the ways they did (unless you scored perfect M46 Dad, of course!). We completely relate and understand that this exercise can be very affirming or very painful, and sometimes both, depending on the number of kids. Don't take anything personally or get hurt, as tough as that might be. Take any negative evaluation and use it for fuel to become an M46 Dad. Let the truth set you free to be all that God wants you to be as a father.

CRASH 6

THE CUP
Dear rhino dad, have these pages open during the CRASH.

PRE-CRASH PREPARATION

Today's CRASH will equip you with the Tool of Freedom. To get the most out of today's CRASH:

1. Before you get to the meeting place, or as you're waiting for the CRASH to begin, flip back through the previous pages. Remind yourself what we talked about, reread what notes you wrote, and refresh your mind about how the challenge went.

2. If possible, silence your phone and put it away. Focus your full attention on being equipped to be the dad your children deserve.

3. Make sure you are fully present by saying a short prayer simply asking the Lord to clear your mind and give you "ears to hear" what you need today to prepare you to lead your family.

4. Be open and transparent with other men at your CRASH. Receive the help you need from another dad and/or provide encouragement to another dad as you both walk this fatherhood journey.

REVIEW AND TABLE TIME

Write down some of the main points from last session's review.

What came up in the discussion that you'd like to commit to pray about? Anything you can do to encourage one of the men at your table?

VIDEO NOTES

As you watch today's video, write down the main points.

IMAGE

The following image is provided to help you remember the main principle of this session and also to help you reteach this to your children or friends.

KEY SCRIPTURE

"For in him the whole fullness of deity dwells bodily, and you have been filled in him, who is the head of all rule and authority."
Colossians 2:9–10

Paraphrase the passage in your own words.

THE TOOL

Each CRASH, we're putting a new tool in your hands. A tool is a principle that can guide your parenting.

In the sixth session, you have been handed the Tool of Freedom. As you will see in this session, we are taking the concept of the four basic needs (L.A.W.S.), and we're giving you and your kids a practical tool that will help you apply this in a very real way.

The image of the cup can be a powerful tool in helping your kids see how the gospel actually allows them to live in real freedom. There is no need to ask that others complete them in any way. Children of God are no longer needy. The more we trust that we are truly complete in Christ, the less we will feel the need for others to fill our cup.

THE CHALLENGE

Dad, you are the most influential man in your child's life. Once again, this is an opportunity for you to use your own story to help bring this truth home for your kids.

CRASH COURSE 6

Dear rhino dad, use the following pages to help you dig deeper into this session and record the challenge as you fight for the hearts of your children. Go through them at your own pace or just pick and choose which to do.

"I can forgive, but I cannot forget, is only another way of saying, I will not forgive. Forgiveness ought to be like a cancelled note—torn in two, and burned up, so that it never can be shown against one."

Henry Ward Beecher

THE HEART OF A RHINO

In 1517, Martin Luther drew up his ninety-five theses condemning the corrupt practices of the Catholic Church in his day. Someone once said that it was as if Luther had climbed up in the steeple and rung the church bells for the whole world to hear. Regardless of what you think of Luther or the Reformation, you have to admit that what happened next is pretty remarkable.

In 1521, Luther was excommunicated by the pope and ordered to appear before the emperor at the Diet of Worms (a religious assembly held in the German city of Worms) to recant what he had written. His life was on the line. Execution was a very real possibility and prison was a certainty—unless he recanted.

Luther refused to recant or rescind his positions. He was told to sleep on it before he made his final decision. He slept on it, and the next day he famously said:

> Unless I am convinced by the testimony of the
> Scriptures or by clear reason (for I do not trust
> either in the pope or in councils alone, since it is
> well known that they have often erred and contra-
> dicted themselves), I am bound by the Scriptures
> I have quoted and my conscience is captive to the
> Word of God. I cannot and will not recant any-
> thing, since it is neither safe nor right to go against
> conscience. May God help me. Amen.[7]

What kind of man would make such a courageous stand? Was it pride? Arrogance? I believe it was that Martin Luther knew what sustained him and made him complete. With all of that pressure to fold and just give in to fit in, Luther stood his ground. He said it himself: "My conscience is captive to the Word of God."

Rhino dad, the Word of God is a person. If you are His, you are complete. You are not needy. And as a dad, you get to do something that will prepare your kids for life in this crazy world like nothing else can.

You get to teach them that they are not walking through life in need of anything. They, too, are complete in Christ. You get to teach them that how they feel doesn't determine what's true.

Just think of the pain this can save them. Just think about how this can impact who they choose to spend their life with. Just think about the impact a man, woman, or kid like that can have for the sake of the gospel.

DIGGING DEEPER

Just as in the L.A.W.S. session, it's helpful to answer the question "How do I know I have all the love, acceptance, worth, and security I need in the person of Jesus?"

If you are a child of God, it sometimes *feels* like your cup is not full—but if you are a child of God, your cup actually is full. The process of sanctification is partly about God convincing you and me more and more that all our needs are already met in Christ. And once God convinces us of that truth, *then* our feelings and our thoughts will, over time, change, as well.

Rhino dad, your children will sometimes feel that they are in need of more love, acceptance, worth, and security. And if they are a child of God, they need to know that's not true. They need to know that there is an enemy who will lie to them and try to convince them that they need to reach outside of Christ to find those needs met. And they need to know how their own flesh operates.

How can you use your own story to help your kids see this illustration come to life?

In what ways, when you were their age, did you reach for L.A.W.S.?

How does this illustration help you to better understand forgiveness?

Is there someone you need to forgive? In what way did that person make you feel like your cup was not full?

What do you need to do to forgive them?

What do you think it might do for your children for them to see that their father is not needy, not easily offended, and knows who he is in Christ?

RHINO COLLISION
Examining your own heart

LEARNED FROM MY DAD

Dads are teaching their children how to live, but they are also "painting a picture of God" with their daily actions. The same is true in your relationship with your own dad.

As we think about the Tool of Freedom, let's take a look at what your father taught you. Ask yourself the following questions and be brutally honest.

This isn't about bashing your father. He did the best he could with what *he* had been given. This is about calling things what they are and assessing the toolbox we walked into fatherhood carrying.

Thinking back on your relationship with your father, do you remember feeling like you wanted something from him that you couldn't get? Attention, words of affirmation, affection, and so on?

What did your dad teach you about where you are to find your identity?

Was your father a forgiving man or a grudge holder?

LEARNED FROM MY CULTURE

Colossians 2:8 (NIV) commands us, "See to it that no one takes you captive through hollow and deceptive philosophy, which depends on human tradition and the elemental spiritual forces of this world rather than on Christ."

We are shaped not only by what we were taught by our father but also by our culture. Ask yourself the following questions and be brutally honest.

What does our culture say about how we should get what we need?

What does our culture say about being respected, saving face, and so on?

Why do you think true forgiveness is so shocking to witness?

What messages have you received about the issues discussed in this _session from the church or from Christians?

A WORD FROM PASTOR TIM

One of the unexpected implications of both this session and the L.A.W.S. session is how these truths can radically transform the way we see other people. My youngest son, Ezra, used to tell me often about a particular kid in school who was always belittling other kids. He was a big dude, and everyone was afraid of this guy. One day, my son said, "Dad, I realize now that he's just starving for respect and wants everyone to think he's awesome." Ezra started seeing this kid in a whole new light. He began to have compassion for him and even befriended him when it seemed no one else would.

Here's the thing: once your kids get a grasp of this concept, they will begin to see this at work all around them. Obviously, this isn't about passing judgment on others. In fact, I believe there's a specific process that God will take us through as we mature.

> 1. God will teach you to see Him through the lens of the gospel.

If you observed God in the Old Testament alone, you might come away with the idea that He's an angry, vengeful God. He seems to be smiting a whole lot of folks. But if you look at God through the lens of the Gospels, you'll see that He is in fact holy and hates sin, but He took His wrath out on His own Son.

Those who are in Christ are "hidden with Christ in God" (Col. 3:3). "For our sake he made him to be sin who knew no sin, so that in him we might become the righteousness of God" (2 Cor. 5:21). God sees you as a son and heir, if you are indeed in Christ. Once you see God through that lens, everything changes.

> 2. God will teach you to see yourself through the lens of the gospel.

If you and I were to be compared to a holy God based on our behavior and thought life, we'd come up short every single time. If we spent our time only comparing ourselves to other people, we could become either full of pride or full of self-loathing. But if we see ourselves through the lens of the gospel, or as God sees us, we can't hold on to pride or self-loathing. Our hope is in Jesus, never in us.

> 3. God will teach you to see others through the lens of the gospel.

If you (or your kids) do an honest assessment of where you stand before God apart from the finished work of Jesus, you may start having more compassion on others. It will be very difficult to ever judge anyone else again. As you interact with people, even difficult people, you will begin to understand that they are 1) complete in Christ and know it, 2) complete in Christ and *don't* know it, or 3) not complete in Christ because they have no access to Him (i.e., they are unsaved).

Why do sinners sin? Well, that's who they are: they are sinners. Why do Christians sin and sometimes hurt other people? Well, because we're not finished yet.

We don't get to judge others, especially other Christians, because we have no idea why they are doing what they are doing or why they are reaching for what they are reaching for. Obviously, within the body of Christ, we have to call sin *sin*. But we don't do that from a position of pride, since we know full well how much we've been forgiven and how we ourselves compare to a holy God.

But, man, what would the world be like if followers of Jesus actually saw beyond the surface in others and became people of grace, patience, and forgiveness?

REWRITING YOUR STORY

Regardless of what your father gave you and what your culture has handed to you, you can be a cycle breaker for good. It's time to be *intentional* about what you will pass down to your children.

Ephesians 4:32 says, "Be kind to one another, tenderhearted, forgiving one another, as God in Christ forgave you." What have you been forgiven?

What, if anything, would you like to see change in how you exhibit forgiveness and long-suffering with your kids?

A father paints a picture of God in the minds of his children. But if Dad is a grudge holder or keeps a record of wrongs, what picture of God will that paint for his children?

What is it that makes it so difficult sometimes to forgive others or to exhibit patience and compassion?

RHINO CHARGE
Fighting for the hearts of your children

Use the space below these Scripture references to record what the
Lord shows you.

Colossians 2:10

Colossians 3:3

John 1:12

Romans 6:6

1 John 3:1–2

2 Corinthians 5:21

A WORD FROM COACH KENNY

I remember the first time Tim taught this session at our local CRASH. A man came up to me right after it was over. I knew him. He was known for having something of a quick temper. "I now understand why I feel like I absolutely have to be respected by everyone," he said. "By my wife, my kids, my students I teach! I now realize that I don't see my cup as full. I am looking for others to fill my cup. I have a need to be respected."

This man was so right. In fact, if you think back to the Tool of Parenting Styles, this session will help you understand questions such as …

- Why does the Best Buddy Dad feel that he has to be liked by his children?
- Why is the AWOL Dad completely emotionally detached from his children?
- Why does the Drill Sergeant Dad feel like he has to be respected and feared by his children?

What a simple but powerful image Tim gives us in this session: a cup. Rhino dad, can't you just see a picture in your mind of a beggar holding out his cup pleading for others to fill it? I can't stand the thought of being an emotional beggar ... but I get absolutely sick to my stomach at the thought of my children being emotional beggars pitifully looking to anyone to fill their cup.

Rhino dad, who is going to teach your children that they have emotional needs that must be met? Who is going to teach your children that God is the One who created those needs so they can be fulfilled only in a relationship with Him? Who is going to teach your children that in Christ their emotional cup is full?

If *you* don't tell them, who will?

Rhino dad, pick up a cup and fight for the hearts of your children!

M46 MOMENT

I (Tim) once heard of a dad who always had to have the best of everything. He had a really nice house in a great part of town. He drove an expensive, decked-out truck. He wore the nicest clothes. He hung out with only those people who would elevate his standing in the community. He golfed at the best courses, and he always posted the best vacation pics on social media.

The problem was, he was nearly bankrupt. His wife was about to come apart over their debt. It was all a sham ... all driven by his need for respect, acceptance, and affirmation. He was a professing follower of Jesus who was so needy that he nearly wrecked his own family just so others would see him a certain way.

When his oldest son graduated from high school, he couldn't afford to pay for the college his son wanted to go to. He also couldn't buy him the nice car he wanted even though all his friends were getting new cars for graduation. His son resented him, and the dad started feeling resentment toward his son for making him feel bad all the time.

It all came to a head when he bailed his son out of jail after he got a DUI. When they got home, they got into a heated argument and that eighteen-year-old boy took a swing at his dad. It was about to get really ugly when Mom stepped in and, in tears, broke up what was about to be a fight.

This dad told me that he went into his basement that night and sobbed like a baby. All he could see in his mind was his little boy's face, the one he'd played catch with all those years in the backyard, the one who used to crawl up in his lap when it was storming outside. And now it had come to this.

He cried out to God and ended up having the sweetest time with Jesus in his basement that he'd ever had. He woke his son up in the middle of the night and just hugged him and cried. He owned his role in creating his son's worldview.

This man's life has been radically changed by the gospel. It took some painful dark nights of the soul, but he let go of what we call "cultural Christianity." He was able to let go of his need for everyone to think he was a hotshot. He downsized everything. To this day, he's trying to undo the damage that was done to his kids and his marriage. His oldest son is a work in progress, but he loves his son deeply.

"Tim," this man recently said to me, "I taught my son arrogance and entitlement, and then I was shocked when he began to act arrogant and entitled."

I nearly cried when he said that to me. His entire countenance had changed, and I could see the evidence of God working on his soul. God is good.

THE CHALLENGE: FIGHT FOR THEIR HEARTS!

"In the future, when your children ask you,
'What do these stones mean?' tell them."

Joshua 4:6–7a (NIV)

Document your challenge here. The more detailed you are, the more you will be able to look back and tell your children the story of God's faithfulness in your life.

Rhino dad, you are the most influential man in your child's life. Be courageous. Tell your kids about how you sometimes hold your cup out for others to fill. Be specific.

Do you find yourself needing recognition from a superior at work? Is there someone that you have had a hard time forgiving? Do you sometimes feel disrespected? Help your kids know that this isn't just something that people deal with when they are young, but it can cripple us all the days of our lives unless the gospel transforms us.

Ask your kids to really examine their hearts and see how they might be holding that invisible cup out for others to fill. Get them to be specific about relationship issues, or how they find themselves needing attention, respect, or credit, or how they desire to fit in.

Remind them (from CRASH 4) exactly how we can know that we have all the L.A.W.S. that we need in Christ.

Tell them that you want to help them, over time, to know and experience more and more that God's children are complete. Remind them that it doesn't feel that way very often, but it's true nonetheless.

Pray with them and ask God to help them remember and recognize that their flesh will always look to find instant gratification. God wants to make us free by spiritually bringing us to maturity. You can't be emotionally needy and spiritually mature at the same time. True spiritual maturation comes with being less and less emotionally needy and more and more secure in who we are in Christ!

CRASH 7

ENCOURAGEMENT VS. EXASPERATION

Dear rhino dad, have these pages open during the CRASH.

PRE-CRASH PREPARATION

Today's CRASH will equip you with the Tool of the Power of the Tongue. To get the most out of today's CRASH:

1. Before you get to the meeting place, or as you're waiting for the CRASH to begin, flip back through the previous pages. Remind yourself what we talked about, reread what notes you wrote, and refresh your mind about how the challenge went.

2. If possible, silence your phone and put it away. Focus your full attention on being equipped to be the dad your children deserve.

3. Make sure you are fully present by saying a short prayer simply asking the Lord to clear your mind and give you "ears to hear" what you need today to prepare you to lead your family.

4. Be open and transparent with other men at your CRASH. Receive the help you need from another

dad and/or provide encouragement to another dad
as you both walk this fatherhood journey.

REVIEW AND TABLE TIME

Write down some of the main points from last session's review.

What came up in the discussion that you'd like to commit to pray
about? Anything you can do to encourage one of the men at your table?

VIDEO NOTES

As you watch today's video, write down the main points.

IMAGE

The following image is provided to help you remember the main principle of this session and also to help you reteach this to your children or friends.

KEY SCRIPTURE

"The tongue has the power of life and death."
Proverbs 18:21 (NIV)

Paraphrase the passage in your own words.

THE TOOL

Each CRASH, we're putting a new tool in your hands. A tool is a principle that can guide your parenting.

In the seventh session, you have been handed the Tool of the Power of the Tongue. When we were kids, there was a saying that went something like "Sticks and stones may break my bones, but words will never hurt me." But do you know that Scripture actually says the exact opposite? Proverbs 12:18 says that reckless words pierce like a sword! Dad, if I told you that you already possessed something, and how you shared it with your children would dramatically impact their opportunity for success or failure in life ... would you want to know what it is? Of course you would! By the way, it's not how much is in your bank account, or your level of education, or even how many connections you have ... it is your tongue! Dad, how we consistently speak to our children will either speak life into them (encouragement) or suck life out of them (exasperation).

THE CHALLENGE

Dad, you are the most influential man in your child's life. Take some time to write down each child's unique qualities, characteristics, talents, skills, gifts, spiritual gifts, and fruit of the Spirit. On a regular basis, speak these to your children.

Fight for the hearts of your children!

CRASH COURSE 7

Dear rhino dad, use the following pages to help you dig deeper into this session and record the challenge as you fight for the hearts of your children. Go through them at your own pace or just pick and choose which to do.

"The essence of parental love is recognizing that we are the dispensers of God's grace into our children's lives. They learn to identify and reference God's character through the way we treat them both in moments of profound pride and in times of intense disappointments."

Bryan Chapell

THE HEART OF A RHINO

In his book *Habitudes*, Dr. Tim Elmore tells the story of a boy who grew up in Europe about a hundred years ago. His father's actual name was Alois Schicklgruber. Growing up, this boy and his father had a terrible relationship. The father was short-tempered and cruel.

For a few years, the boy went to a Catholic monastery school. The young boy was said to have a beautiful voice and was part of the school choir. Because of this wonderfully positive experience, the boy wanted to become a priest, but the father relentlessly ridiculed him for this, and eventually the boy quit considering it.

As the young boy grew, he later decided he wanted to become an artist. He had great skills in drawing and watercolor paints. Once again, the father ridiculed the idea of being an artist. After his father's death, the young man applied to enter the Vienna Academy of Fine Arts, but he was rejected. For the next few years, he scratched out a living as a watercolor painter.

When World War I broke out, he volunteered for the military, and this set him on his future path. "He decided to put up an emotional wall," Dr. Elmore writes, "and never let anyone inside his heart. He ran away. The boy grew up to be a man. The man became a leader. You know him as Adolph Hitler."[8]

This is obviously an extreme story of the results of a father's exasperation, but there is a very real lesson for us to learn here. Colossians 3:21 (NASB) says, "Fathers, do not exasperate your children, so that they will not lose heart." There is a frightening result that occurs when a child feels that they just simply can never measure up. They give up!

DIGGING DEEPER

In the video, I (Kenny) discuss how it is so easy for me to go into "Coach Mode" at home, barking orders without much consideration of feelings. I think most dads who work in environments where productivity is a priority can easily exasperate their children without realizing it or intending to do so.

Here are six "exasperators" we must watch out for in communication with our children:

1. Unrealistic Expectations

We must not communicate to our kids that our love is performance-based. As a coach, I see this all the time—performance directly connected to praise or criticism, with no in-between.

2. Comparison to Peers

We can be guilty of constantly comparing our children to other kids—or, even worse, a successful sibling. That rejection can be devastating and permanently damaging for them.

3. Instruction without Encouragement

Once again, as a coach, I have been guilty of this one far too often. The desire to just drive, drive, drive, and point out the path to improvement without ever stopping to praise or encourage can create a great deal of negative baggage in any child.

4. Intrusions and Impositions

For busy and stressed-out dads, children can be seen only as life interruptions. Their constant questions and requests can become noise to us that interferes with everything "important," from a business call to a TV show. The constant treatment of "You're just in my way" can wear a kid down until he or she feels worthless.

5. Pushing to Grow Up Too Fast

Today's culture can easily usher kids straight from childhood into adulthood, skipping adolescence. Smartphones, technology, social media, and cultural media bring children face-to-face with adult issues far too soon and much too often.

6. Overprotection

The other side of the challenge in not pushing our children to grow up too fast is to avoid becoming what family counselors call a "helicopter parent." That parent *hovers over* their children constantly,

smothering and not allowing conflict or consequences to occur so
they can grow and mature.[9]

Using the six "exasperators," ask some tough questions of yourself. Rhino dad, work hard to put yourself in your child's shoes.

Where am I placing unrealistic expectations on my kids?

Where am I comparing my kids to anyone else?

Where am I constantly instructing my kids with little or no
encouragement?

Where am I treating my kids like they are intrusions and impositions?

Where am I pushing my kids to grow up too fast?

Where am I overprotecting and hovering over my kids?

RHINO COLLISION
Examining your own heart

LEARNED FROM MY DAD

Dads are teaching their children how to live, but they are also "painting a picture of God" with their daily actions. The same is true in your relationship with your own dad.

As we think about the Tool of the Power of the Tongue, let's take a look at what your father taught you. Ask yourself the following questions and be brutally honest.

This isn't about bashing your father. He did the best he could with what *he* had been given. This is about calling things what they are and assessing the toolbox we walked into fatherhood carrying.

Thinking back to your father … in what way(s) did your father encourage you? How did that affect you?

Thinking back to your father … in what way(s) did your father exasperate you? How did that affect you?

LEARNED FROM MY CULTURE

Colossians 2:8 (NIV) commands us, "See to it that no one takes you captive through hollow and deceptive philosophy, which depends on human tradition and the elemental spiritual forces of this world rather than on Christ."

We are shaped not only by what we were taught by our father but also by our culture. Ask yourself the following questions and be brutally honest.

What does our culture say about encouraging children?

What does our culture say about exasperating children?

How do most of your peers talk to their kids in terms of exasperation or encouragement? How does that affect you?

What messages have you received about encouragement and exasperation from the church or from Christians?

A WORD FROM PASTOR TIM

In my earlier days as a dad, I did not do well in this area. And most of my friends seemed to have the same parenting style. With four boys (all of them playing sports year-round), a crazy household, and school on top of that, I'm sure I exasperated more than I encouraged.

I think I believed that if I could instill just enough fear in them to get them to conform at home, perform on the field, and excel in the classroom, I had done my job as a father.

I took them to church, of course. But if they got a picture of God from me, then their picture was that of a very demanding God who expected external conformity above all else. I love my boys, and it wasn't my intention to harm them in any way. But, looking back, I know that my words, and even sometimes my looks, made them fearful and constantly off-balance about where they stood with me.

If I could go back in time, that's one thing I would change for sure. I'd be very intentional about it. I've talked through all of this with my boys, and we've had honest discussions about who I was then and who I am now. One clear fact has emerged from those conversations: I was not painting a very appealing picture of God for them to see.

By the way, I was a Sunday school teacher and vice chairman of the deacons back in those days. My boys saw lots of religious activity in my life, and very little of God.

As dads, we can get so busy and focused that we ramp up our expectations on everyone else around us. If we could see the way we chip away at the souls of those we love when we fail to encourage, we'd make some adjustments. Our prayer is that this chapter will give you the motivation to take a hard, honest look at encouragement vs. exasperation and go through with the challenge.

REWRITING YOUR STORY

Regardless of what your father gave you and what your culture has handed to you, you can be a cycle breaker for good. It's time to be *intentional* about what you will pass down to your children.

Proverbs 18:21 says the tongue can speak both life and death. How are you currently speaking both life and death into each of your children? Remember that you have a unique relationship with each child.

What, if anything, would you like to see change in how you speak to your children?

A father paints a picture of God in the minds of his children. On this topic, what kind of brush are you using and what kind of picture of God are you painting for your kids?

When it comes to encouragement vs. exasperation, how do you react to this sentence: "The power of the tongue holds life and death"?

Going forward, how can you intentionally speak life into your children?

RHINO CHARGE

Fighting for the hearts of your children

Use the space below these Scripture references to record what the Lord shows you.

Colossians 3:21

Judges 6:1–16

James 3:3–6

Proverbs 12:18

Psalm 19:14

Ephesians 4:29

A WORD FROM COACH KENNY

In an earlier session, we discussed how our flesh is composed of a mind (thinker), a heart (feeler), and a will (chooser). Over time, our flesh takes on baggage that we come to believe about ourselves, especially if it is spoken by someone close to us.

I have met many men who have heard their fathers say terrible and untrue things to them that they have taken on as truth: "You will never amount to anything," "You are a loser," or "You are a mistake." That list can, unfortunately, go on and on. In the video, I mention the heartbreaking story of a four-year-old who thinks his name is "Idiot" because he has been called that so much. It is so true that "the words of the reckless pierce like swords" (Prov. 12:18 NIV).

But Proverbs 18:21 reminds us that the tongue holds not only the power of death but also the power of *life*. Is that true? Is it possible that regular dads could have the power to speak life and death into their kids?

In Judges 6, we meet a man named Gideon. Gideon describes himself this way: "My clan is the weakest in Manasseh, and I am the least in my father's house" (v. 15). Gideon describes himself as literally the weakest man he knows! In fact, when we meet Gideon in Judges 6, he is hiding from the Midianites. Left to himself, we can only conclude that Gideon would never see himself as anything more than a weak nobody … the weakest man in all the land.

But God sends an angel with a very direct message for Gideon: "The LORD is with you, mighty warrior" (v. 12 NIV). He also tells him to take an army and free Israel from the Midianite oppression. *What?*

I am not saying that your kids are Gideon and you are God's angel. But you most certainly are God's messenger sent by Him to *speak life* to your children!

Rhino dad, the way you handle the power of the tongue in each of your children's lives could change everything for them.

What if, instead of reminding them of their faults, mistakes, and shortcomings, you consistently reminded them of their true identity in Christ? What if you replaced your disapproving words with the message that they are not weak but are more than conquerors? What if they started hearing from you that they are not defined by past mistakes but are covered by the blood of the Lamb? That they are not in bondage to sin but are redeemed? That they are not bound by law but abound in grace? What if what they heard you saying was that they are never alone but are much-loved children of the most-high King?

Rhino dad, begin to intentionally speak life into your children … and ignite a revolution in your own home.

M46 MOMENT

Over the years, Tim and I have seen many examples of how the hearts of fathers and children have been turned toward each other. This session is one that seems to do that quite often. Here are two of my favorite M46 Moments from this session.

A few years ago, I (Kenny) was teaching this session in a CRASH Community. When I neared the end, one of the dads raised his hand. It was a dad who had never spoken up before, so I was immediately interested in what he would say.

He said his son was a senior in high school who had recently made a stupid mistake that had cost him a full scholarship at a prestigious university. The dad shared with the entire group of men that morning that, in his anger and frustration, he had been relentless in telling his son how disappointed he was and questioning him over and over how he could have made such a dumb mistake.

As the dad spoke, he shared that he knew in his spirit that his communication had gone from truthfulness to shaming his son. With tears in his eyes, this dad told the group that he knew he needed to immediately leave, go tell his son how much he loved him, that he still believed in him, and that he would walk with him through this tough time side by side.

I will never forget listening to this dad proclaim his love for his son and watching him literally stand up to fight for the heart of his son! The man left that room with the encouragement of all his rhino brothers.

The second story involves the challenge to put your hands on your children and pray for them. Several years ago, a couple of weeks after teaching this lesson, I had a dad call me. He told me that after coming to M46 and hearing this session, he realized he had never actually placed his hands on his children and prayed for them out loud. This dad expressed to me that for some reason he felt uncomfortable doing that, but he made the decision that he would simply be intentional.

He decided that, every morning before his children left for school, he would put his hands on them and pray for them individually. This dad shared with me that it went from feeling uncomfortable to something he looked forward to each day. He said that he didn't understand why, but it seemed to have completely opened up his relationship with his kids. He said that there was now a closeness that they'd simply not had before.

What a beautiful illustration of Malachi 4:6: "And he will turn the hearts of fathers to their children and the hearts of children to their fathers."

THE CHALLENGE: FIGHT FOR THEIR HEARTS!

"In the future, when your children ask you,
'What do these stones mean?' tell them."

Joshua 4:6–7a (NIV)

Document your challenge here. The more detailed you are, the more you will be able to look back and tell your children the story of God's faithfulness in your life.

Rhino dad, you are the most influential man in your child's life. Take some time to write down each child's unique qualities, characteristics, talents, skills, gifts, spiritual gifts, and fruit of the Spirit. On a regular basis, speak these to your children. Pray them into their lives as you pray for and over them. Find some creative ways (like below) to remind them of the amazing things God has placed into them.

1. Plan nights for an individual outing with each of your kids. Take your child out for a special evening. It doesn't have to cost anything. What you do is up to you. During this dedicated and intentional time, tell your child the unique and special qualities that you see that God has placed inside of them.

2. Speak life into your children before bedtime or before they leave for school by placing your hands on them and praying. Speak words of blessing and encouragement through your prayer.

3. The next time your child does something wrong or does anything he or she considers to be a failure, instead of dropping "the dad hammer," show grace and speak their true identity to them, just as God did for Gideon. In moments of weakness, speak warrior words.

Then the LORD said to Moses, "Tell Aaron and his sons to bless the people of Israel with this special blessing: 'May the LORD bless you and protect you. May the LORD smile on you and be gracious to you. May the LORD show you his favor and give you his peace.'" (Num. 6:22–26 NLT)

Fight for the hearts of your children!

CRASH 8

THE BATTLE CRY
Dear rhino dad, have these pages open during the CRASH.

PRE-CRASH PREPARATION

Today's CRASH will equip you with the Tool of Biblical Courage. To get the most out of today's CRASH:

1. Before you get to the meeting place, or as you're waiting for the CRASH to begin, flip back through the previous pages. Remind yourself what we talked about, reread what notes you wrote, and refresh your mind about how the challenge went.

2. If possible, silence your phone and put it away. Focus your full attention on being equipped to be the dad your children deserve.

3. Make sure you are fully present by saying a short prayer simply asking the Lord to clear your mind and give you "ears to hear" what you need today to prepare you to lead your family.

4. Be open and transparent with other men at your CRASH. Receive the help you need from another dad and/or provide encouragement to another dad as you both walk this fatherhood journey.

REVIEW AND TABLE TIME

Write down some of the main points from last session's review.

What came up in the discussion that you'd like to commit to pray about? Anything you can do to encourage one of the men at your table?

VIDEO NOTES

As you watch today's video, write down the main points.

IMAGE

The following image is provided to help you remember the main principle of this session and also to help you reteach this to your children or friends.

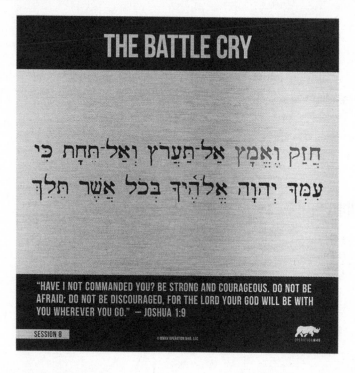

KEY SCRIPTURE

"Have I not commanded you? Be strong and courageous. Do not be afraid; do not be discouraged, for the LORD your God will be with you wherever you go."

Joshua 1:9 (NIV)

Paraphrase the passage in your own words.

THE TOOL

Each CRASH, we're putting a new tool in your hands. A tool is a principle that can guide your parenting.

In the eighth session, you have been handed the Tool of Biblical Courage. In this session, we examine the calling of Joshua and how that relates to us as fathers.

Joshua was clearly called by God to lead his people into the Promised Land. God was also clear that there would be great opposition: terrifying situations, complaining people, hostile forces, and more. God called on Joshua to be strong and courageous, not based on Joshua's confidence in himself, but because Joshua could have the confidence that God was with him.

The same is true with us as fathers. God has clearly called each of us to be not only the providers and protectors of our children but also the spiritual leaders (priests) of our home. And, like Joshua, we will face plenty of opposition along the way. God has called us and God is with us. The only question is whether we will *advance* and take the land.

THE CHALLENGE

Dad, you are the most influential man in your child's life. One way to model Christlike servant leadership and priesthood to your children, while also setting your family's feet on firm ground, is to volunteer and minister together. Lead them in service.

Fight for the hearts of your children!

CRASH COURSE 8

Dear rhino dad, use the following pages to help you dig deeper into this session and record the challenge as you fight for the hearts of your children. Go through them at your own pace or just pick and choose which to do.

> *"A true soldier fights not because he hates what is before him, but loves what is behind him."*
>
> G. K. Chesterton

THE HEART OF A RHINO

I (Kenny) hate fear! It has made me make bad decisions in my life. What I have found is that in certain times in my life, I just did not have enough courage to overcome that fear.

"Fear has a tendency to masquerade itself as indecision, caution, or even as false wisdom," says Pastor Steve Berger. "When we don't face our fear, we rehash choices that have already been made. We question our decisions."

I hate to admit this, but there have been a few times in my life when fear has gripped me to the point where I became indecisive, unsure, and unable to make a decision. As I look back, I think I understand why that happened.

For many years, I completely misunderstood courage. When I was young, I thought courage was about not having any fear. I would watch movies of great superheroes and warriors who seemed not to be afraid of anything.

As I got older (and a bit wiser to TV and movies), I realized that not to have any fear was a terrible definition for courage. In fact, it was probably a better definition for stupidity. I mean, if I did not have a healthy fear of fire, I would just put my hand in a flame. A healthy fear of getting hit by vehicles keeps me from jogging down the middle of the interstate. Having "no fear" is a very poor definition of courage.

My new definition of courage was having the willingness to face your fears. That worked for a while, but I eventually saw that, while it's a much better definition than the first, it still had major problems. As I got older, I found that some things I must face in life are just way bigger than me.

It wasn't until studying the life of Joshua that I realized what true biblical courage was. God said to Joshua, "Be strong and courageous. Do not be frightened, and do not be dismayed, for the LORD your God is with you wherever you go" (Josh. 1:9). I had spent so much time trying to be "strong and courageous" that I never realized where godly courage came from.

Biblical courage does not come from the strength of my body, the intelligence of my brain, the compassion of my heart, or the power of my will. God's kind of courage comes from the bold assurance of knowing that God is with me. What I needed (and what we all need) is *faith*. Faith allows me to compare my challenges to something greater than my strength, my intelligence, my heart, and my will. Faith allows me to compare my challenges to God!

Jesus said, "I have said these things to you, that in me you may have peace. In the world you will have tribulation. But take heart; I have overcome the world" (John 16:33). As a believer, you have the opportunity to approach every situation from a position of victory rather than fear. In other words, we fight *from* victory, not *for* victory.

That is biblical courage and it changes everything!

DIGGING DEEPER

In Joshua 1:3, God tells Joshua, "Every place that the sole of your foot will tread upon I have given to you." The Lord had commanded Joshua to lead his people into the Promised Land. He had even told Joshua that He would be with him every step of the way.

What is interesting, though, is that God also made it clear that Joshua would face massive opposition. Joshua would conquer the land, but only those portions of the land that his boots took. Consider the task and opposition that stood before him: a river at flood stage, a complaining people, thirty-one hostile nations waiting to attack him. I am sure Joshua must have felt underprepared, underqualified, and even downright fearful of the responsibility. But God wasn't going to do this for him. Joshua had to advance and take the land.

Rhino dad, the same is true with you and me as fathers! In His Word, God has clearly called fathers "to do" a number of things. He has also declared that He will be with us in those tasks. At the same time, God also makes clear that there will be plenty of hardships, challenges, and opposition. I do not mean to sound unspiritual, but there are a number of things that we simply do not have to pray about, because God has already revealed His will about them.

Rhino dad, you don't have to pray and ask God if you should be the spiritual leader of your home. God has already declared in Scripture that you are (see Heb. 12:9–11 and Eph. 6:4, for example). He's not changed His mind on that over the centuries. The only question now is whether or not you will *advance* and take that land.

Just as God's will was clearly for Joshua to lead the Israelites, His heart for you is to be the priest of your own home and the spiritual leader for your family. You can have bold confidence that He is with you as you fight for the hearts of your children.

As the spiritual leader of your home, here are some things that God has already spoken for you to do:

- God has called you to teach your children.

And you must commit yourselves wholeheartedly to these commands that I am giving you today. Repeat them again and again to your children. Talk about them when you are at home and when you are on the road, when you are going to bed and when you are getting up. (Deut. 6:6–7 NLT)

- God has called you to discipline your children.

Fathers, do not provoke your children to anger by the way you treat them. Rather, bring them up with the discipline and instruction that comes from the Lord. (Eph. 6:4 NLT)

- God has called you to guide your children.

The godly walk with integrity; blessed are their children who follow them. (Prov. 20:7 NLT)

- God has called you to love your children.

Love is patient and kind. Love is not jealous or boastful or proud or rude. It does not demand its own way. It is not irritable, and it keeps no record of being wronged. It does not rejoice about injustice but rejoices whenever the truth wins out. Love never gives up, never loses faith, is always hopeful, and endures through every circumstance. (1 Cor. 13:4–7 NLT)

• God has called you to serve with your children.

So fear the LORD and serve him wholeheartedly.… But as for me and my family, we will serve the LORD. (Josh. 24:14, 15 NLT)

• God has called you to protect your children.

Those who respect the LORD will have security, and their children will be protected. (Prov. 14:26 NCV)

• God has called you to be proud of your children.

Children are a gift from the LORD; they are a reward from him. Children born to a young man are like arrows in a warrior's hands. How joyful is the man whose quiver is full of them! (Ps. 127:3–5a NLT)

• God has called you to leave a legacy for your children.

The good man's children will be powerful in the land; his descendants will be blessed. (Ps. 112:2 GNT)

• God has called you to pray for your children.

Pour out your hearts like water to the Lord. Lift up your hands to him in prayer, pleading for your children. (Lam. 2:19 NLT)

- God has called you to have compassion for your children.

As a father has compassion on his children, so the LORD has compassion on those who fear him. (Ps. 103:13 NIV)

- God has called you to turn your heart toward your children.

And he will turn the hearts of fathers to their children and the hearts of children to their fathers. (Mal. 4:6)

RHINO COLLISION
Examining your own heart

LEARNED FROM MY DAD

Dads are teaching their children how to live, but they are also "painting a picture of God" with their daily actions. The same is true in your relationship with your own dad.

As we think about the Tool of Biblical Courage, let's take a look at what your father taught you. Ask yourself the following questions and be brutally honest.

This isn't about bashing your father. He did the best he could with what *he* had been given. This is about calling things what they are and assessing the toolbox we walked into fatherhood carrying.

Thinking back to your father, what did you learn from him about being the spiritual leader of a home?

Thinking back to your father, what did you not learn from him about being the spiritual leader of a home?

LEARNED FROM MY CULTURE

Colossians 2:8 (NIV) commands us, "See to it that no one takes you captive through hollow and deceptive philosophy, which depends on human tradition and the elemental spiritual forces of this world rather than on Christ."

We are shaped not only by what we were taught by our father but also by our culture. Ask yourself the following questions and be brutally honest.

What does our culture say about a father being the spiritual leader of the home?

How are most of your friends doing as the spiritual leader of their homes? How does that affect you?

What messages have you received about being the spiritual leader of your home from the church or Christians?

A WORD FROM PASTOR TIM

Kenny Dallas is a football coach. I've listened to him do his pregame thing in the locker room. Those young players run out of that locker room ready to crash through walls if they have to. He's really good at inspiring people. Everywhere Kenny has coached, he has had great success.

But during the week at practices, he and the other coaches spend a lot of time making sure those kids know where to go when the ball is snapped. This is more than a rah-rah lesson. This is about doing what you need to do even when you don't feel like it.

We've met with a lot of dads over the years. So many of them either feel ill-equipped to be the dad they want to be or they feel they have done so much damage that they have lost the credibility they need to turn things around with their kids.

You and I can't forget that God is with us and in us. God absolutely wants to use you as a force for good in the lives of your kids, no matter what has happened in the past.

A theme I've noticed in God's Word is that, aside from creating the world and raising Jesus from the dead, most everything God does, He does through people. Broken, imperfect people.

God parted the Red Sea for the Israelites to escape the Egyptian army—but He had Moses raise his staff first. Jesus healed the blind man in John chapter 9—but He first rubbed mud on his eyes and told him to go wash it off. Was there something magical about Moses's staff? Was that magic mud? Of course not! God wanted to engage people in what He was doing.

In the same way, He wants *you* to join Him in what He's wanting to do in the minds and hearts of your children. Kenny gave some really good practical steps you can take, but *you* have to take the steps. You really can be bold and courageous, because it's not on you. It's on Him. But, rhino dad, you get to be the person God uses. Remember, you are the spiritual leader in your home!

REWRITING YOUR STORY

Regardless of what your father gave you and what your culture has handed to you, you can be a cycle breaker for good. It's time to be *intentional* about what you will pass down to your children.

If you had to give yourself a score from 0–100 on how intentional you are being as a spiritual leader in your home, what score would you give yourself, and why?

The majority of Christian men are not the spiritual leaders in their home because they feel apprehensive, unprepared, or fearful. What is it that tends to hold you back?

A father paints a picture of God in the minds of his children. On this topic, what kind of brush are you using and what kind of picture of God are you painting for your kids?

When it comes to this subject, how do you react to this sentence: "To be a better dad, God needs to be bigger in your heart and in your house"? Knowing that God is with you as you lead your family, how might God become bigger in your heart and house?

RHINO CHARGE
Fighting for the hearts of your children

Use the space below these Scripture references to record what the Lord shows you.

Joshua 1:1–11

Proverbs 11:14

Proverbs 29:18

Psalm 127:3–5

A WORD FROM COACH KENNY

I once read a story about how elephants were kept in camps by using small pieces of rope tied to their legs. A trainer explained why the elephants didn't even try to break free from this bit of string. "When they are very young and much smaller, we use the same size rope to tie them. At that age, it's enough to hold them. As they grow up, they are conditioned to believe they cannot break away. They believe the rope can still hold them, so they never try to break free."[10]

What we learn when we are young absolutely affects us when we're grown. The truths we believe—both good and bad—are like iron cords in our minds, and we usually don't even question them.

This reminds me of Psalm 127:4 (NIV): "Like arrows in the hands of a warrior are children born in one's youth." Each of us knows how an arrow works. It's nocked to the string, pulled back, held against the bow, pointed in a certain direction, and shot. But what happens to an arrow if there is no bow?

More than one in four children in America are growing up in fatherless homes. That's 19.7 million children, according to the 2017 US Census. But at M46, we are just as concerned with children growing up in homes where the father may be physically present but spiritually absent. There is no clear vision or direction being provided by the one whose job it is to lead his family.

Years ago, when my oldest children were very young, I was fortunate enough to read a book called *Wild at Heart*. In this and later books, author John Eldridge says that it is the father's role to answer a fundamental question that every child is asking: "Do I have what it takes?" If a father does not answer that question, the child grows up with a void in his soul, always seeking that answer.

As a young father, I understood that it was my role to provide a vision for my children. They were arrows in the hands of a warrior. What would I do?

I made a decision that I wanted my children to hear me *speak life* into them every day. I decided that, every night, as my children went to bed, I would give them a vision of who they were in Christ and what they could be. I determined that this would be the last thing they would hear me say every day.

Every night, when my boys were tucked into their bed, each of them would hear me say these words: "Son, one day you will be a mighty man of God. Whatever you do, do it with all your heart, as if working for the Lord and not for man. I love you with all my heart. You have what it takes!"

I never realized what a big deal this was to my sons until the first time I had to go out of town after starting this nightly tradition. "Daddy," they said, "how are you gonna be able to say 'Mighty Man' to us if you leave?" I have made plenty of parenting mistakes over the years, but in that moment, I realized how important it was for my children to hear me say "Mighty Man" to them every day.

Rhino dad, can you imagine what could happen in your family if you became intentional about being the spiritual leader of your home? Those arrows in your home need to be aimed and shot! Rhino dad, it is time for us to *advance* and take the land!

M46 MOMENT

One of my (Kenny's) favorite M46 Moments happened immediately after teaching this session. I was part of a CRASH that met from 6:30–7:30 a.m. At noon of that day, I had a dad reach out to me to share something I will never forget.

This dad told me that during our CRASH the thought hit him that he had *never* heard his dad tell him that he loved him. He said that he thought as hard as he could, but he couldn't remember a single time. But then, things got much worse for him. He said as he sat there, he couldn't remember a time where he had ever told his own children that he loved them!

The dad then shared with me that, after the CRASH was over, he went to his car and sat in the parking lot crying for two hours. When he called me at noon, he told me this story, but it didn't end with him alone in the parking lot. He boldly declared to me, "I know

I probably got this from my dad, and he probably got this from his dad, but it ends with me! From now on, I will tell my kids 'I love you' every day of their lives."

THE CHALLENGE: FIGHT FOR THEIR HEARTS!

"In the future, when your children ask you,
'What do these stones mean?' tell them."

Joshua 4:6–7a (NIV)

Document your challenge here. The more detailed you are, the more you will be able to look back and tell your children the story of God's faithfulness in your life.

Rhino dad, you are the most influential man in your child's life. One way to model Christlike servant-leadership and priesthood to your children, while also setting your family's feet on firm ground, is to volunteer and minister together. Lead them in service.

Depending on the age of your children, here are a few suggestions of places where you can serve:

- Children's hospital
- Nursing home
- Food pantry
- Homeless shelter
- Offer childcare for a single mom
- Repair work for an elderly widow

Embrace your role as the physical protector and financial provider of your home. But advance to take the ground to be the priest and spiritual leader of your family, as well. God is with you as you fight for the hearts of your children.

Then the King will say to those on his right,
"Come, you who are blessed by my Father, inherit
the Kingdom prepared for you from the creation of
the world. For I was hungry, and you fed me. I was
thirsty, and you gave me a drink. I was a stranger,
and you invited me into your home. I was naked,
and you gave me clothing. I was sick, and you cared
for me. I was in prison, and you visited me."

Then these righteous ones will reply, "Lord,
when did we ever see you hungry and feed you?
Or thirsty and give you something to drink? Or a
stranger and show you hospitality? Or naked and
give you clothing? When did we ever see you sick
or in prison and visit you?"

And the King will say, "I tell you the truth,
when you did it to one of the least of these my
brothers and sisters, you were doing it to me!"
(Matt. 25:34–40 NLT)

Fight for the hearts of your children!

RECONCILING RHINOS

Dear rhino dad, have these pages open during the CRASH.

PRE-CRASH PREPARATION

Today's CRASH will equip you with the Tool of Modeling Grace. To get the most out of today's CRASH:

1. Before you get to the meeting place, or as you're waiting for the CRASH to begin, flip back through the previous pages. Remind yourself what we talked about, reread what notes you wrote, and refresh your mind about how the challenge went.

2. If possible, silence your phone and put it away. Focus your full attention on being equipped to be the dad your children deserve.

3. Make sure you are fully present by saying a short prayer simply asking the Lord to clear your mind and give you "ears to hear" what you need today to prepare you to lead your family.

4. Be open and transparent with other men at your CRASH. Receive the help you need from another

dad and/or provide encouragement to another dad
as you both walk this fatherhood journey.

REVIEW AND TABLE TIME

Write down some of the main points from last session's review.

What came up in the discussion that you'd like to commit to pray
about? Anything you can do to encourage one of the men at your table?

VIDEO NOTES

As you watch today's video, write down the main points.

IMAGE

The following image is provided to help you remember the main principle of this session and also to help you reteach this to your children or friends.

KEY SCRIPTURE

"Therefore, if anyone is in Christ, the new creation has come: The old has gone, the new is here! All this is from God, who reconciled us to himself through Christ and gave us the ministry of reconciliation: that God was reconciling the world to himself in Christ, not counting people's sins against them. And he has committed to us the message of reconciliation."

2 Corinthians 5:17–19 (NIV)

Paraphrase the passage in your own words.

THE TOOL

Each CRASH, we're putting a new tool in your hands. A tool is a principle that can guide your parenting.

In the ninth session, you have been handed the Tool of Modeling Grace. This session is all about challenging you, rhino dad, to model the love and grace of Jesus by being a minister of reconciliation. This tool is about helping you teach your kids that followers of Jesus are like soldiers or firemen: they run toward the danger and the mess, not away.

THE CHALLENGE

Dad, you are the most influential man in your child's life. We're assuming you don't want your kids to grow up to be people who are all about their own comfort and their own good all the time. You want to see your kids' lives transformed by the gospel. You want to see them grow up to be men and women whose hearts are captivated by Jesus.

CRASH COURSE 9

Dear rhino dad, use the following pages to help you dig deeper into this session and record the challenge as you fight for the hearts of your children. Go through them at your own pace or just pick and choose which to do.

> *"You may choose to look the other way but you can never say again that you did not know."*
> William Wilberforce

THE HEART OF A RHINO

"Time and again," wrote Dane Ortlund in *Gentle and Lowly*, "it is the morally disgusting, the socially reviled, the inexcusable and the undeserving, who do not simply receive Christ's mercy but to whom Christ most naturally gravitates. He is, by his enemies' testimony, the 'friend of sinners' (Luke 7:34)."[11]

It's truly fascinating to read through the Gospels. Jesus always seems to tell stories that make the wrong person the hero. It's the immoral younger brother, not the responsible older brother. It's the misfits, the prostitutes, the woman caught in adultery. It's never the super-religious. Literally, never.

This is the God we're following. Jesus' actions throughout the New Testament demonstrate that He is patient and kind, gentle and lowly. He's drawn toward contrition and repelled by pride. Yes, He is holy, but that doesn't stop Him from running toward the broken and contrite.

So, rhino dad, how do we introduce this Jesus to our children?

Dietrich Bonhoeffer was born into an aristocratic family in Germany in 1906. As a young child, he was such a good pianist that his family assumed he'd go into music. But at the age of fourteen, he announced that he intended to become a minister and theologian.

He graduated from the University of Berlin in 1927. Adolf Hitler became chancellor of Germany in 1933. Bonhoeffer began teaching at an underground seminary, openly speaking out against Hitler. He began trying to help Jews escape Nazi oppression. And he eventually joined a plot to overthrow or even assassinate Hitler.

You can't overestimate the groupthink that was prevalent in Germany at this point in history. Anyone who didn't go with the Nazi flow was ostracized, and many were imprisoned. But Dietrich Bonhoeffer was driven by something more than blending with the crowd. He stood with those who were being targeted for their race, and he became a target himself.

Bonhoeffer actually visited America as a guest lecturer in the late 1930s. He wrote a letter back to a friend, saying, "I have made a mistake in coming to America. I must live through this difficult period in our national history with the Christian people of Germany. I will have no right to participate in the reconstruction of Christian life in Germany after the war if I do not share the trials of this time with my people."

Though his American friends were pleading with him to stay put, he returned to Germany. In April 1943, Bonhoeffer was arrested and sent to Tegel Prison. He spent two years there, writing to family and friends and pastoring fellow prisoners. He was eventually transferred to Buchenwald, and then to the extermination camp at Flossenburg. On April 9, 1945, one month before Germany surrendered, he was hanged with six other resisters.

Here is the account of the execution from the perspective of a camp doctor who witnessed the scene:

> The prisoners ... were taken from their cells, and
> the verdicts of court martial read out to them.
> Through the half-open door in one room of the
> huts, I saw Pastor Bonhoeffer, before taking off
> his prison garb, kneeling on the floor praying
> fervently to his God. I was most deeply moved by
> the way this lovable man prayed, so devout and so
> certain that God heard his prayer. At the place of
> execution, he again said a prayer and then climbed
> the steps to the gallows, brave and composed. His
> death ensued in a few seconds. In the almost 50
> years that I have worked as a doctor, I have hardly
> ever seen a man die so entirely submissive to the
> will of God.[12]

Dietrich Bonhoeffer followed Jesus. He didn't worry about
what the masses thought about him. He gave his life rather than go
along with the ideas that would have kept him safe.

DIGGING DEEPER

If you are a child of God, you are a minister of reconciliation. That
means you get to be used by God as He reconciles people back to
Himself. You also get to be used by God to restore those who have
stumbled into sin and created pain for themselves and others.

The earthly consequences of sin can be devastating. But Jesus
ran toward those who were broken and contrite. And in Luke 15,
in the prodigal son story, we see the father pleading with his *older*
son, who was prideful and defiant. One of the profound points of
that parable is that God wants to restore not only those people who
are self-loathing and broken but also those who are self-righteous
and prideful.

For some reason, in many church environments, the self-righteous and prideful guy is seen as noble and less sinful. "At least he's trying really hard." But when we see the outwardly sinful and obviously unrighteous guy, we think we need to pull him aside and have a talk with him. Neither of those guys is a product of the gospel, and God wants to restore both to Him. If you are following Jesus, just remember that He is going to lead you where others won't go.

Rhino dad, the following questions are not about producing shame for you. This is all about helping you to become a minister of reconciliation.

Why do you think Christians sometimes shun or avoid those who are caught in sin?

What might the one who is caught in sin be thinking or feeling about God or the church?

What might that person need from you?

Have your children ever heard you share the gospel with someone? If so, describe that time (or one of those times). If not, what are your thoughts on the topic?

In the past, have your children heard you gossip or speak in a derogatory way about someone who has fallen into sin or whose life has fallen apart because of their own decisions? How might that impact the way your children see God?

Are you okay with your children becoming a friend of sinners? What does that mean? What does that not mean? What do you think that looks like for them?

How can you encourage your kids to be ministers of reconciliation at school, at work, or wherever they are?

RHINO COLLISION
Examining your own heart

LEARNED FROM MY DAD

Dads are teaching their children how to live, but they are also "painting a picture of God" with their daily actions. The same is true in your relationship with your own dad.

As we think about the Tool of Modeling Grace, let's take a look at what your father taught you. Ask yourself the following questions and be brutally honest.

This isn't about bashing your father. He did the best he could with what *he* had been given. This is about calling things what they are and assessing the toolbox we walked into fatherhood carrying.

Thinking back on your relationship with your father, did you see him as someone who was all about other people?

Did he go out of his way to help others, even those who were shunned by other people, or broken?

Describe an instance when your father exhibited the ministry of reconciliation.

How did your father talk about outcasts, those who failed, or those who made a mess of their lives?

LEARNED FROM MY CULTURE

Colossians 2:8 (NIV) commands us, "See to it that no one takes you captive through hollow and deceptive philosophy, which depends on human tradition and the elemental spiritual forces of this world rather than on Christ."

We are shaped not only by what we were taught by our father but also by our culture. Ask yourself the following questions and be brutally honest.

What does our culture say about the way we should treat failures and people who make a mess of their lives?

What does our culture say about the kind of people we should be seen associating with?

What is it about our culture that contributes to the kick-'em-when-they're-down mentality?

What messages have you received about the issues discussed in the Reconciling Rhinos session from the church or from Christians?

A WORD FROM PASTOR TIM

Jesus ran toward people with broken, contrite hearts. Can that be said of you and me? Are we gaining the reputation of being a friend of sinners? Are we seen as men who rescue and reconcile? Do we stand with the shunned and the shamed when everyone else is slinging mud?

It's never too late, rhino dad. We can model the heart of Jesus for our kids, but only if He is transforming us. And if your kids see the gospel at work in you, they are far more likely to follow Jesus.

REWRITING YOUR STORY

Regardless of what your father gave you and what your culture has handed to you, you can be a cycle breaker for good. It's time to be *intentional* about what you will pass down to your children.

What obstacles prevent us from treating hurting, broken, and sinful people the way Jesus did?

What, if anything, would you like to see change in how you model grace for your kids?

A father paints a picture of God in the minds of his children. What kind of picture of God are you painting for your kids in modeling grace?

RHINO CHARGE
Fighting for the hearts of your children

Use the space below these Scripture references to record what the
Lord shows you.

2 Corinthians 5:18

Colossians 3:12

2 Corinthians 1:3–4

John 8:1–11

Galatians 6:1

2 Corinthians 2:7

A WORD FROM COACH KENNY

Did you know that 88 percent of children who grow up in our churches will leave the faith after high school graduation?[13] As a father of six children and a teacher and coach in Christian schools for the last twenty-plus years, I absolutely *hate* that number. But it is also why I love that Tim is challenging each of us to become a reconciling rhino ... and to do it in front of our children for them to see.

Texas pastor Matt Chandler says, "Our job is not to save our children. Our job is to teach them about Jesus, putting as much kindling around their hearts as we possibly can so that the Holy Spirit can come in and ignite the fire."

As awful as that 88 percent statistic is, let me give you another stat from Jerry Pipes. Jerry has been a youth minister for over thirty years. In his experience, when a child grows up in a home where the mother and father have been actively modeling their faith and are engaged in ministering to people, that number drops to as low as 5 percent.

You know what this tells me? It tells me that there are a lot of great people who can help me raise my children—the church, youth ministers, godly teachers, godly coaches, and more—*but there is no substitute for you.*

What do your children need to see from you? They need to see that your faith is real. They need to see your faith is about action and not just words. Your children need to see your love for Christ through the way you model grace and love others.

Rhino dad, the Tool of Modeling Grace for your children is so important. Tim taught us that this tool is like the Marines or firemen running directly toward a problem while all others run away. Your children need to see a faith in you that is lived out and real by the way you love and serve others. Your children need to see you run *toward* problems and not away from them. They need to see a reconciling rhino!

Rhino dad, you hold the paintbrush and you are painting a picture of God for each of your children. Be a reconciling rhino and paint for them a true picture of God, who loves us so much that He is always running toward us!

M46 MOMENT

Daniel had grown up in a Christian home, but his parents divorced when he was young. Daniel was angry and directionless after that. He was especially angry with his dad. When he got older, Daniel got into drugs and alcohol and found himself homeless and living in the woods. He lived this way for years, and he lost all contact with his family. There was a seething resentment in his heart, and he blamed his dad for everything.

One day, Daniel left the woods he was living in and walked almost twenty miles to a convenience store in town. While Daniel was standing in the store, to his astonishment, his father walked in. His own father walked right past him and said, "Excuse me," as he brushed by. Daniel was furious and humiliated. He felt the rejection all over again.

After his father left the store, Daniel began to text his dad. Years of anger and vitriol came pouring out in his texts. When his father responded, Daniel was shocked to learn that his father had been out looking for him. "You walked right past me in the store." But Daniel had lost so much weight and had been so physically consumed by his drug use that his own father didn't even know who he was.

His dad asked him if he could get to a hotel. Daniel said he could. His father paid for the hotel on the phone and then met him in his room. He pleaded with his son to let him take him to a rehab facility. Daniel agreed, but later he started having second thoughts. He decided to sneak out in the middle of the night and go get high at least one more time.

When he got to the parking lot, he ran in to more relatives, who had been summoned to help. They took him back up to the room. Several of Daniel's family members slept on the floor of that hotel room that night to ensure that Daniel got the help he needed.

Daniel's life has now been totally transformed by the gospel. The people in his life who know Jesus ran after him when he didn't even want to be found. I (Tim) have sat in my office and listened to Daniel's powerful story. We even recorded his story on video and played it on a recent Easter Sunday. Daniel is a different man today. He and his father have more than restored their relationship. And Daniel can't keep quiet about the reconciling love of Jesus.

THE CHALLENGE: FIGHT FOR THEIR HEARTS!

"In the future, when your children ask you,
'What do these stones mean?' tell them."

Joshua 4:6–7a (NIV)

Document your challenge here. The more detailed you are, the more you will be able to look back and tell your children the story of God's faithfulness in your life.

Rhino dad, you are the most influential man in your child's life. If you're reading this, then more than likely you would describe yourself as a follower of Jesus. You're not a perfect follower, and neither am I, but you're a follower.

The next time you're reading the Gospels, imagine that you're literally following Jesus around as He lived His life and interacted with people. Jesus went where others wouldn't go. He talked to people others wouldn't be seen talking to. He befriended people others had shunned. He defended people others wanted to bash.

Jesus wasn't into groupthink. He didn't care if His actions would benefit Him socially or not. He often risked His own reputation for the good of others … so much so that people began to say He was a glutton and a drunkard. Not because He was, but because He was around such people enough to be associated with them.

I once heard someone say, "You know you're becoming more like Jesus when you're gaining the same reputation He had.… He was a friend of sinners."

This time, the challenge is pretty simple: become a minister of reconciliation and take your kids along for the ride.

Talk with your children about the biblical idea of being a minister of reconciliation. Tell them the stories of how Jesus ran toward the broken (the adulterous woman, Zacchaeus, etc.). Give them an example of a time when someone was a minister of reconciliation in your life. Help your children to recognize people in their own lives that they could model grace for.

Most importantly, ask God to help you to become a proactive minister of reconciliation, and allow your kids to see you modeling grace for others.

Fight for the hearts of your children!

CONCLUSION

Rhino dad, we really hope this journey through these M46 Dads CRASH courses has been beneficial to you. From the very beginning, this ministry has had two basic goals: to inspire and equip fathers to fight for the hearts of their children, and to help dads experience and communicate to their kids the difference between pursuing religion and being transformed by the gospel.

There is no greater responsibility than being a father. And to be a truly great father, it requires gospel transformation and real intentionality. Back in CRASH 1, the Finish Line, we determined that the most important thing in this life is our relationship with God. If that's true, then that's the most important area in which we need to influence our kids.

But if we just hand over to our kids a dead religion of fear-motivated behavioral modification, then all we've done is placed an incredibly heavy burden on their shoulders, a burden "that neither our fathers nor we have been able to bear" (Acts 15:10b). All that will do is cause them to resent, and maybe even hate, God. At a minimum, they will become disillusioned.

Jesus came to set us free from condemnation, fear, and religion. He wants us to find joy and life in Him. He wants His children to know, deep down in their bones, that He loves them. And He wants His children to live from that place.

But, rhino dad, you can't give something away that you don't have. If Christianity is just a religious pursuit for you, then that's all you'll have to give to your kids. As dads, we have the incredibly unique responsibility of introducing our children to who God is and what He's like.

Remember, you are the greatest influence in the lives of your children. Nothing—not church attendance, peers, media, youth pastors, or anything else—can usurp your influence in the lives of your children. For better or worse, the mark you leave on the souls of your children will be profound.

M46 Dads is all about equipping dads to clearly *communicate* and *demonstrate* the gospel and the love of God to their children. It's not about perfection; it's about progress. God works even through our failures and our weaknesses. As fathers, we're going to fail to be all that we want to be in the lives of our children. For some of us, that failure may be significant. But God redeems. He really does reconcile and restore. If we own our failures, walk in humility, and let Him teach us along the way, He can do incredible things.

Our children are going to fail, as well. But those are the best teachable moments. How do we respond to our children when they fail? How does the gospel inform the way we walk through failure with them?

God really is good, rhino dad. No matter where you're starting from, He can heal, restore, and teach. Our prayer—not just today, but for the rest of your life—is that you embrace this life in Christ, engage your will, advance to take ground, and fight for the hearts of your children.

NOTES

1. Robert Lewis, *Winning at Work and Home* (Nashville: LifeWay), n. p.

2. Part of the inspiration for the rhino analogy is from *The Barbarian Way* by Erwin McManus (Nashville: Thomas Nelson, 2005), 96–97.

3. Larry Taylor, *Running with the Horses: A Parenting Guide for Raising Children to Be Servant-Leaders for Christ* (Bloomington, IN: WestBow Press, 2013), 33.

4. Mark D. Griffiths, "Why We Seek the High of Stardom," *Psychology Today*, March 24, 2014, www.psychologytoday.com/us/blog/in-excess/201403/why-we-seek-the-high-stardom.

5. John Ericson, "Incredible Self-Surgeries in History: Do-It-Yourself Procedures Include Appendectomy, Amputation," Medical Daily, August 27, 2013, www.medicaldaily.com/incredible-self-surgeries-history-do-it-yourself-procedures-include-appendectomy-amputation-254751.

6. See also two early published papers on prototypes by D. Baumrind: "Effects of Authoritative Parental Control on Child Behavior" (1966), *Child Development*, 37(4), 887–907; and "Child Care Practices Anteceding Three Patterns of Preschool Behavior" (1967), *Genetic Psychology Monographs*, 75(1), 43–88.

7. "Luther at the Imperial Diet of Worms (1521)," Luther.de, accessed August 4, 2020, www.luther.de/en/worms.html.

8. Tim Elmore, *Habitudes: Images That Form Leadership Habits and Attitudes* (Atlanta: Poet Gardner, 2014), n. p. See also: "The History Place: The Rise of Adolph Hitler," History Place, www.historyplace.com/worldwar2/riseofhitler/index.htm; and "Adolph Hitler: Man and Monster," BBC, www.bbc.co.uk/teach/teach/adolf-hitler-man-and-monster/zbrx8xs.

9. At the time of this publishing, we could not locate the original source that inspired this list of items, but we will keep searching and will happily add it to future reprints.

10. Marie Fay, "The Elephant and the Rope," Inspirational Storytellers, February 27, 2013, http://inspirationalstorytellers.com/the-elephant-and-the-rope/.

11. Dane Ortlund, *Gentle and Lowly: The Heart of Christ for Sinners and Sufferers* (Wheaton, IL: Crossway, 2020), 27.

12. "Dietrich Bonhoeffer: German Theologian and Resister," *Christianity Today*, accessed August 4, 2020, https://www.christianitytoday.com/history/people /martyrs/dietrich-bonhoeffer.html.

13. Jerry Pipes and Victor Lee, *Family to Family: Leaving a Lasting Legacy* (Alpharetta, GA: North American Mission Board of the Southern Baptist Convention, 1999), 50. The 88 percent drop-out figure is from Jay Strack's experience among the nation's top student ministry leaders (similar studies varied from 75 percent to 91 percent).